CLB 4896
This edition published in 1996 by CLB Publishing for
Siena Books
a imprint of Parragon Book Service Ltd
Unit 13-17 Avonbridge Trading Estate, Atlantic Road
Avonmouth, Bristol BS11 9QD
This compilation © 1996 CLB Publishing
© Eaglemoss Publications Ltd 1996
All rights reserved
ISBN 0-7525-1722-8
Printed in Hong Kong

PICTURE CREDITS

Photographs: Allsport 6, 24(t), 62(bl), 138; Charles Briscoe-Knight 96, 164; Colorsport 165(tr); Peter Dazeley **front cover (centre right)**, 4, 122, 128, 165(r); Matthew Harris 158, 162, 165(br); Mark Newcombe 140; Phil Sheldon Photo Library 24(b), 70, 84, 92, 94, 134, 135, 136; Yours in Sport 25, 86, 167
All other photographs by Eaglemoss/Phil Sheldon

Illustrations: Mike Clark, Kevin Jones, Chris Perfect/Egg Design

LOWERING
— YOUR —
HANDICAP

SIENA

•CONTENTS•

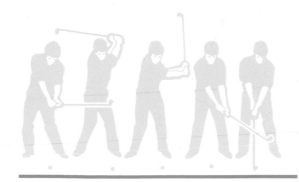

• INTRODUCTION •

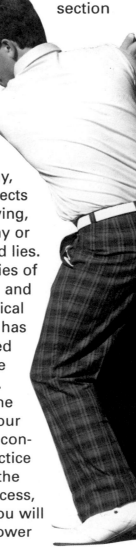

Golf is a game that requires a unique combination of physical skill, mental concentration and a real desire for success. Its constant challenges, unique unpredictability and the fact that players never stop learning, no matter what their level of proficiency, fascinates all who have succumbed to its allure.

For those devoted to improving their game, *Lowering Your Handicap* becomes an instructional manual. Each section concentrates on a particular aspect of play, illustrating the techniques required as well as showing you how to modify your approach when faced with those real-life situations. The details of each technique are shown in the specially commissioned photography, enabling you to improve such aspects of the game as grip, stance and swing, as well as mastering your wood play or helping you recover from awkward lies. We also take a look at the mysteries of putting and the art of bunker play, and offer advice on many other practical elements. *Lowering Your Handicap* has been compiled by two experienced teachers, enabling you to improve your golf in a variety of ways. Avoid reading all the sections in one go, choosing instead an aspect of your game that requires attention and concentrate on improving it on the practice ground before venturing onto the course. There is no short cut to success, but by improving your technique, you will enjoy your game to the full, and lower your handicap in the process.

Alignment Faults

Aligning your body correctly is one of the most vital basics in golf. You swing around your body, so if you're facing in the wrong direction you're unlikely to swing along the proper path.

DEVELOPING A FAULT

To make up for misalignment, your body devises a compensating movement – a fault – to bring the club along the path you want. Although this may work to begin with, your consistency is bound to suffer eventually. By then, the fault has become ingrained in your swing and is much harder to erase.

Make sure you're aligned correctly, so that you can build an orthodox swing. The body – your feet, hips and shoulders – is properly aligned when parallel to the

ARE YOU PARALLEL?
Correct alignment is vital for a proper swing path and smooth body rotation. Use clubs on the practice tee to check your shoulder, hip and feet alignment at address.

Shoulder out of sight
When you're on the course, a simple way of checking alignment is to look at the target and make sure you can't see your left shoulder.

Correctly aligned, your left shoulder should be only just out of sight of your left eye. If you can see it, you're almost certainly aligned right of target.

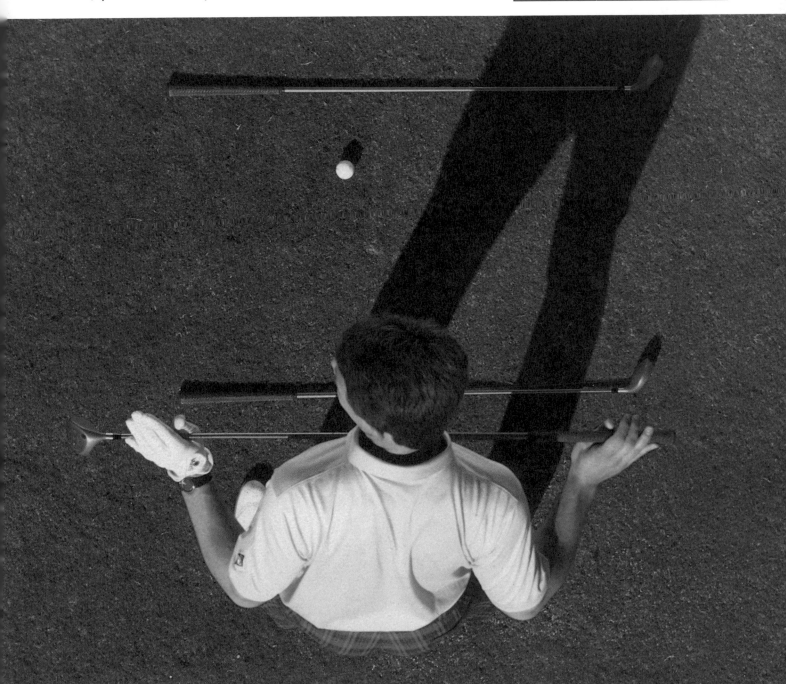

HOW POOR ALIGNMENT CAUSES BAD SHOTS

WRONG – ALIGNING LEFT

A slice can result from aligning yourself too far to the left. You're no longer parallel to the ball-to-target line – your backswing becomes severely restricted because you can't make a full shoulder turn at 90° to your ball-to-target line. This causes you to tilt rather than turn your shoulders. An out-to-in swing path results, making a slice very likely if the clubface is open at impact. Should you close the clubface at impact you pull the ball – it flies immediately left.

It's worth remembering that slicing and pulling are the most common bad shots in golf. At least half the time the root cause is poor alignment.

WRONG – ALIGNING RIGHT

If you align too far to the right of the ball-to-target line, you swing from in to out. This creates too much spin as the club swings across – rather than through – the ball. When the clubface is closed a hook results, while an open clubface causes a push – the ball flies straight to the right.

A slice can also occur, especially with less experienced players. You subconsciously realize at the top of the backswing that you're wrongly aligned and try to adjust. This last minute change causes you to swing from out to in, as you try to pull the club around your body. With a closed clubface in this situation you pull the ball – if it stays open you slice.

ball-to-target line.

The body should face slightly left of target (right of target for left handers). This lets you swing the club easily towards the target without obstruction by your body. Never make the mistake of trying to align your body directly at the target – golf is not like rifle shooting and the clubhead is not as close to your body as a rifle is.

SHOULDERS, HIPS AND FEET

The order of importance in your alignment is shoulders, hips and feet. Your shoulder alignment is crucial because the shoulders begin your body turn. Many players neglect the shoulders in favor of the feet because they can clearly gauge feet position but can't see their shoulders.

Remember that your whole body – for which your shoulder, hips and feet are the check – must be properly aligned, after you've aimed the clubface. You can't swing well if one part is correct and another is wrong. Poor alignment ruins good body turn.

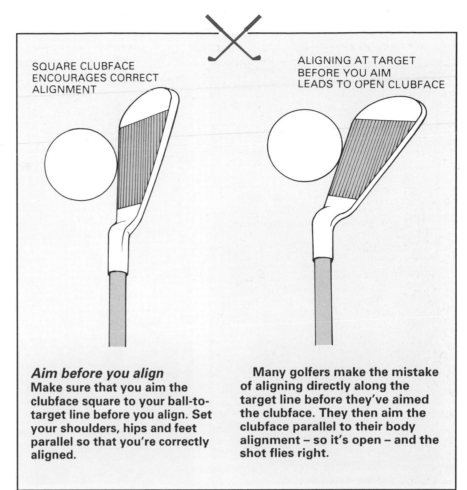

SQUARE CLUBFACE ENCOURAGES CORRECT ALIGNMENT

ALIGNING AT TARGET BEFORE YOU AIM LEADS TO OPEN CLUBFACE

Aim before you align
Make sure that you aim the clubface square to your ball-to-target line before you align. Set your shoulders, hips and feet parallel so that you're correctly aligned.

Many golfers make the mistake of aligning directly along the target line before they've aimed the clubface. They then aim the clubface parallel to their body alignment – so it's open – and the shot flies right.

GOOD ALIGNMENT

CORRECT – ALIGNING SQUARE
Your body is correctly aligned when your shoulders, feet and hips are parallel to the ball-to-target line. Only then can you swing along the correct path and let your body complete its proper turn.

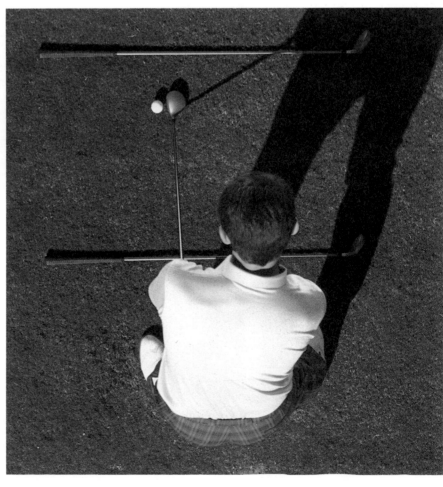

pro tip

Check your alignment
When you're on the practice tee, always pick a target at which to aim. Many players simply whack balls without considering where they want them to fly.

Once you've chosen a target, picture a line running from it through the middle of the ball.

Check the alignment of your upper body to that line by holding your club lengthwise across your shoulders and chest. Then lower the club and lay it along the ground just in front of your feet. Does it run parallel to your ball-to-target line? If it does, your alignment must be correct.

Although you can't carry out this procedure on the course, it's an effective practice tee routine. Many top pros use it, as you'll see if you spend some time watching on the practice tee at a tournament.

HOOKING AND PUSHING

ADDRESS
From a closed stance – when your body is aligned right – you're likely to hook or push the shot.

BACKSWING
You tend to swing the club inside the line early in the backswing causing an in-to-out path.

IMPACT ZONE
The in-to-out path causes a hook if the clubface is closed at impact or a push if the face is open.

Grip Problems

One of the most common faults in golf is a bad grip. Even with a perfect set-up and swing, the ball won't travel absolutely straight if your grip is wrong.

The function of the grip is to return the clubface square to the ball-to-target line at impact. Anything other than a perfect grip results in the ball traveling right or left of the target.

However experienced you are, you should frequently check the position of your hands on the club.

It's easy for a tiny error to creep into your grip without you realizing the change.

CHECK GRIP FIRST

Because most bad grips feel comfortable, many players attribute poor shots to a swing fault. They end up changing their set-up to try and cure the problem but this only makes matters worse – two wrongs don't make a right.

Whenever your game goes sour, start by checking your grip because most faults are caused by a basic error. Only if your grip is correct should you start checking other parts of your game, such as body alignment, stance and ball position. Remember that gripping the club correctly is the most important part of your game.

With the correct grip you see one and a half knuckles on your left hand, while the V between your right thumb and right forefinger points directly at your chin.

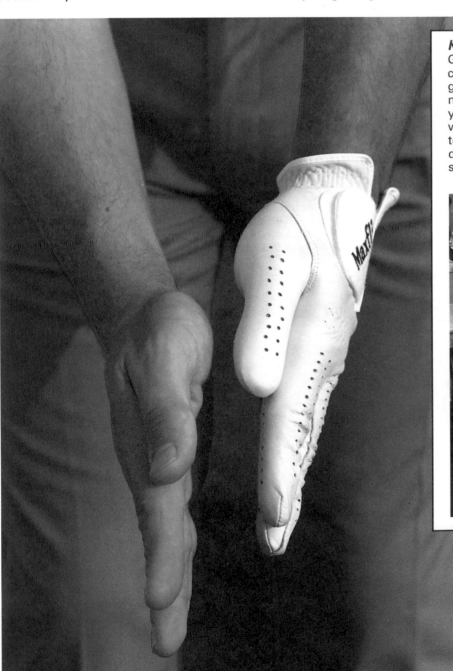

Keep them clean
Give your golf the best start by cleaning your grips regularly. Dirt gets trapped in the ridges of a grip, making it slippery and reducing your hold. Remove all the grime with a brush and soapy water and towel the grips dry. It's very difficult to return the clubface square to the ball if your hands slip.

HANDS SQUARE AT IMPACT
To feel the perfect impact position, take up an imaginary set-up, with your hands stretched out and square to the ball-to-target line. Your hands dictate the position of the clubface. At impact, the back of your left hand, the palm of your right hand and the clubface should be square to the ball-to-target line.

GOOD AND BAD GRIPS

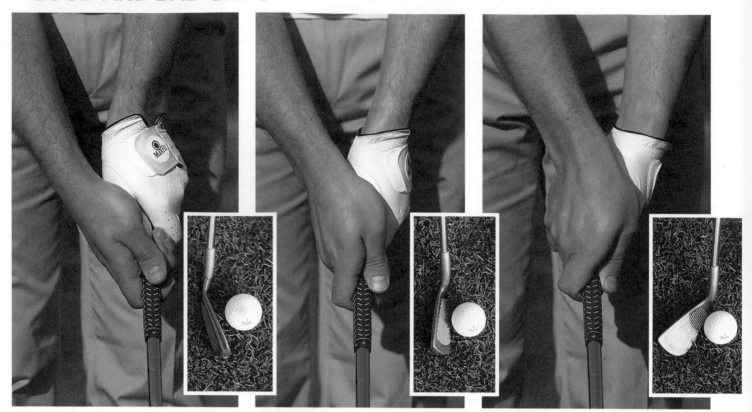

STRONG GRIP
At address you see more than one and a half knuckles on your left hand and the V on your right hand points right of your chin. The clubface is closed at impact, making the ball go left.

CORRECT GRIP
With a perfect grip you see one and a half knuckles on your left hand and the V on your right hand points at your chin. At impact the clubface is square and the ball flies straight.

WEAK GRIP
At address you see one or no knuckles on your left hand and the V on your right hand points left of your chin. The clubface is open at impact and so the ball flies right of the target.

STRONG GRIP

CLOSED CLUBFACE

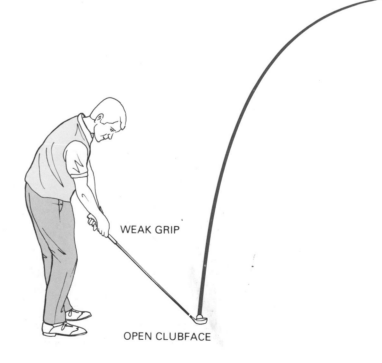

WEAK GRIP

OPEN CLUBFACE

HOOK OR PULL
With a strong grip your hands close the clubface at impact. The ball is hooked or pulled to the left. It's an easier fault than a weak grip to remedy.

SLICE OR PUSH
With a weak grip, your hands fail to square the clubface through impact. It remains open on the downswing and the ball is sliced or pushed to the right.

GETTING TO THE CORRECT GRIP

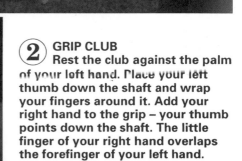

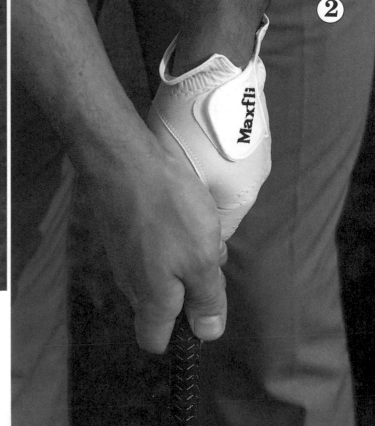

② **GRIP CLUB**
Rest the club against the palm of your left hand. Place your left thumb down the shaft and wrap your fingers around it. Add your right hand to the grip – your thumb points down the shaft. The little finger of your right hand overlaps the forefinger of your left hand.

① **GET HANDS SQUARE**
To get your hands square, adopt a set-up with arms stretched and hands open, your left slightly ahead of your right. At address the back of your left hand and the right palm should be square to a ball-to-target line.

pro tip

Strengthen your fingers
Squeeze a squash ball in the palm of each hand in turn. Repeat the exercise several times a day – strong fingers are an advantage in golf. They help you keep a firm grip of the club

and prevent it slipping in your hands.

If your fingers are weak it's difficult to square the clubhead through impact. The clubface stays open and the ball goes right.

With a bad grip your hands are too much to one side – how far varies. If your hands are too far right your grip is called strong; too far left is known as a weak grip. Strong or weak in this sense doesn't refer to how tightly you hold the club, but describes where your hands are placed on the grip.

THE STRONG GRIP

If you have a strong grip you see more than one and a half knuckles on your left hand and your right hand V points right of your chin.

With a strong grip, your hands automatically close the clubface at impact and the ball swerves to the left. The stronger your grip, the further right your hands – and the ball flies further left.

THE WEAK GRIP

When both your hands are left of the correct position, the V on your right hand points left of your chin and you see less than one knuckle on your left hand.

This prevents your hands naturally squaring the clubhead through impact. The clubface stays open, hitting the ball right of the target. The further left your hands are, the weaker your grip and the further right the ball goes.

A weak grip causes more prob-

lems than a strong grip. Squaring the clubhead through impact is difficult at the best of times – even with the correct grip. A weak grip exaggerates the problem, resulting in a massive slice.

GRIP IT RIGHT

Spend time setting up the basics of a good standard overlap grip. Adopt a normal relaxed stance with your arms and hands stretched out. Set the back of your left hand and the palm of your right hand square to the ball-to-target line.

Keeping your left hand open, take the club firmly in your right hand and place the grip against the palm of your left hand.

Close the fingers of your left hand around the club, with your thumb pointing down the front of the shaft. Make sure there is about a 2in (5cm) gap between the butt (end of the shaft) and your left hand. You should see one and a half knuckles.

Add your right hand to the grip, so that your right thumb covers most of your left thumb and points left of center down the shaft. Let your fingers wrap around the grip with the little finger of your right hand resting on the cleft between forefinger and middle finger of your left hand. Don't grip the club

too tightly. This is the standard overlap grip.

OLD HABITS DIE HARD

Curing a grip fault is harder than you think – particularly if how you hold the club differs greatly from the correct grip. Old habits die hard. It isn't easy to discard a bad grip that feels comfortable, even when you've identified it as the reason your shots travel off line.

The correct grip may feel unnatural at first. But don't be tempted to go back to your old one. Unless you persevere your problems remain.

You'll need lots of practice before you see an improvement. Don't expect your shots to get dramatically better overnight. And don't expect your grip to feel comfortable right away.

Only through constant practice with a correct grip that seems strange to begin with does your new hand position start to feel natural and your shots improve.

The practice grip
This is molded to place your hands and fingers exactly on the grip. If your grip is strong or weak, it helps you become accustomed to the correct grip. Fix a practice grip to an old club and use it regularly until the correct grip feels comfortable and you automatically take it up. But note that it's against the rules to use this aid in competition.

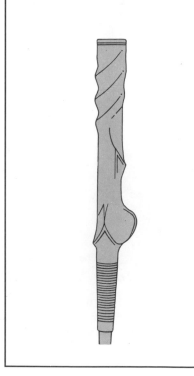

Check your Ball Position

P lacing the ball correctly is one of the most neglected fundamentals in golf. When they play a wayward shot, many players analyze their swings in search of the cause – but faulty ball position could be the culprit.

Being out of place by as little as a ball's width can make all the difference between striking off the heel, toe or sweet spot of the club.

It's all too easy to take your stance so that the ball is too far back or forward – so quickly check where the ball is every time.

STANCE WIDTH

You must strive to use the same swing for all 13 lofted clubs – apart from helping your tempo, it's much easier than having 13 different swings.

To repeat your swing throughout the bag, adjust your ball position and stance width as the club length changes. Your purpose is to hit the ball on the lowest part of your swing with every club – except the woods, which you need to hit on the upswing.

For example, with the long clubs – such as your driver – the ball should be opposite your left heel. It moves nearer your feet and toward the middle of your stance as club length lessens. With the medium irons, the ball is between the center of your stance and your left heel. With the short irons the ball is centered.

Change your stance so that it's widest with the driver and narrowest with the heavily lofted clubs.

PATH AND PLANE

To understand completely the importance of correct ball position it's vital to recognize the part played by swing path and swing plane.

The plane is the angle of your swing path in relation to the ground. It's judged by two things – your height and the distance you

PERFECT PLACING
The ball should always be between two points – opposite your left heel and the center of your stance. This position differs from driver to short iron. Because the face of each club is square to the ball-to-target line only for a split second, it's vital that you set up with the ball in the correct spot.

BALL POSITION – DRIVER

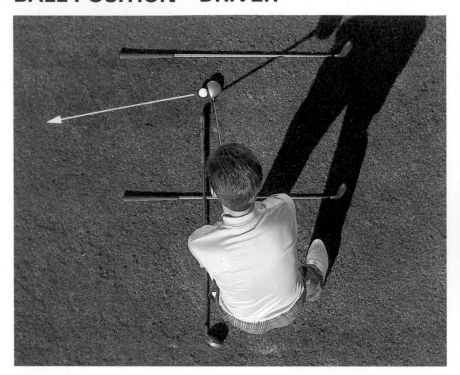

BALL TOO FAR FORWARD
You're likely to hit the ball left, because at impact the clubface is closed and your upper body is open. You may also hit the ball thin (halfway up) because the clubhead makes contact too high on the upswing. The ball probably scuttles along the ground with little power or distance.

▶The white ball is correctly placed opposite the left heel.

WHERE DO YOU PLACE THE BALL?

With the longest clubs – for which you take your widest stance and place the ball furthest away from you – the ideal position for the ball is opposite your left heel. Move the ball nearer the center of your stance – bringing your feet closer together – as club length shortens. The ball should be in the middle of your narrowest stance with the short irons. A normal stance must be square on to the ball-to-target line.

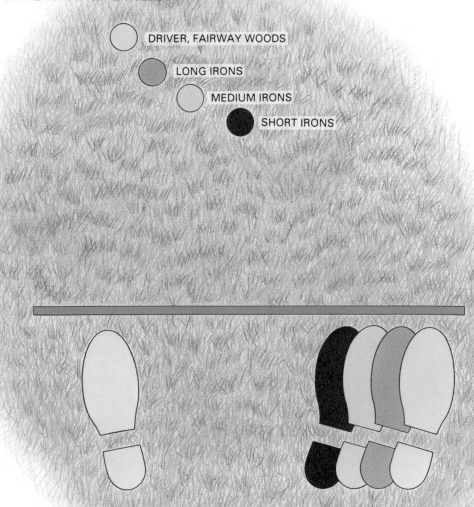

DRIVER, FAIRWAY WOODS
LONG IRONS
MEDIUM IRONS
SHORT IRONS

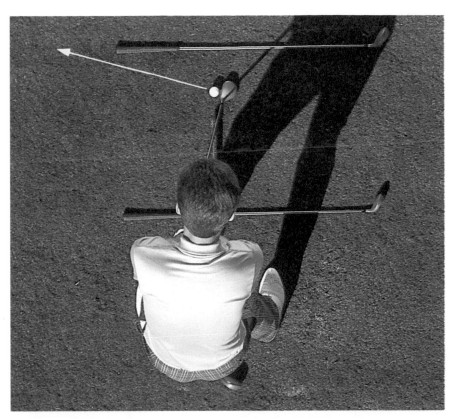

BALL TOO FAR BACK
You hit immediately right because the clubface is open at impact and your upper body is closed. You may strike the ball fat (behind), because the clubhead has not yet reached its lowest point in the swing, and meets the ball too soon. **X**

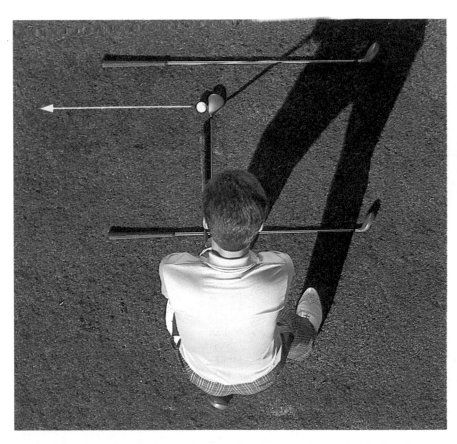

CORRECT – OPPOSITE LEFT HEEL
The proper ball position for a driver is opposite your left heel. You make contact the moment the clubhead begins to rise – which helps the ball gain height – and during the split second when the clubface is square to the target line. **✔**

SET YOUR POSITION: SHORT IRONS

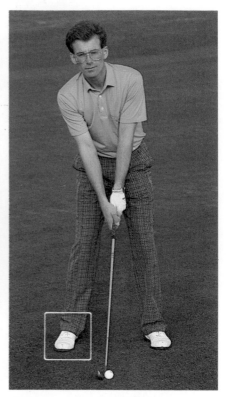

① FEET TOGETHER
Stand with your feet fairly close together and the ball placed exactly in the middle of your stance. Carefully position the clubface square to your ball-to-target line.

② LEFT FOOT POINTS OUT
Keeping your right foot in place, plant your left foot comfortably to one side. The left foot should point slightly outward throughout your swing action to promote an effective and balanced body turn.

③ BALL DEAD CENTER
Move your right foot the same distance from the ball as your left so that the ball is in the center of your stance. Shifting one foot at a time keeps the clubface square and helps you maintain good balance from the outset.

pro tip

Try the hand span test
To make sure that you're standing the correct distance away from the ball, check how far your body is from the top of the club.

After setting up as normal, take your right hand off the club. Place your little finger on your left thigh and your thumb on the butt of the club. A comfortable hand span – neither stretched nor compressed – confirms the correct distance.

When the ball is too far from your body you're likely to hit off the toe of the club, losing power and control. A hook is also probable.

With the ball too near your body the heel of the club strikes the ball, so you may shank. A slice is also a strong possibility.

stand from the ball at address.

When you swing the longer shafted clubs, you stand more upright and slightly further away from the ball than you do with – for instance – an 8 iron. This leads to a flatter swing plane than with the shorter clubs, when you're more bent over.

SPLIT SECOND TIMING

Whatever the club, and whatever the shot, the clubface is square for only a fraction of a second during the swing. That's why ball position is so vital – it must be perfect to receive the clubhead in that split second.

Spend time practicing these changes in stance width and ball position. They must become automatic so that you know you can always swing from a solid base. This skill does not emerge overnight – it may take an entire season before your set-up becomes second nature and your ball position reliable.

Curing Posture Problems

Before you start your swing, you must position your body properly as you address the ball. Correct posture is vital because it is the basis of an effective golf swing. Although you may feel happy with how you stand, faults can creep in easily and cause problems with your game.

Begin by making sure that you're playing with suitable clubs. Their length and lie must suit your height and arm length.

STAND POISED AND READY
Whatever your build and height you should be able to keep faults from creeping into your posture. Stand comfortably at address in almost a semi-sitting position, feeling poised and ready for action. Your back should stay reasonably straight – make sure you don't stoop.

See a qualified PGA pro to check these essentials – without them you have no chance of swinging to your potential. More importantly, you also risk back pain and injury if you strain too many of the wrong muscles.

BE COMFORTABLE

Treat your posture as a way of moving your body into a relaxed, comfortable position, so that you're poised and ready for action. When you get it right, you are perfectly balanced throughout your swing, because your arms, legs and body can move freely and without strain.

If your knees are locked your spine leans over too much, re-stricting your muscle movement. Bending your knees a lot forces you to crouch over the ball, so that making a full shoulder turn is very hard.

YOUR STANCE

Stance is an important ingredient of the correct posture. It promotes balance and helps control. Take your stance by setting the insides of your feet the same distance apart as your shoulders.

Narrow your stance for the shorter clubs and widen it for the longer clubs and woods. Too narrow a stance makes you badly balanced and restricts upper body

SHORT

AVERAGE

TALL

HOW GOOD IS YOUR POSTURE?

GOOD: KEEP MOVING
Correct posture is vital as it is the foundation of a good golf swing. Relax and keep your body moving so that you don't adopt faults. Feel live tension in your arms and legs. Keep your back fairly straight.

GOOD: AT THE TARGET
With a correct posture and a good swing, the club points directly at the target at the top of the backswing. Your lower body must stay flexed and fluid, letting your weight transfer smoothly.

movement.
Point your left foot (right foot if you strike left handed) slightly outwards – it must point in the direction that your body is turning as you strike the ball. Pointing your left foot inwards badly hampers your movement and causes physical strain.

POSTURE EXERCISE

When your stance is sound, you can prepare your posture. The point of changing your body position from its normal upright bearing is to create a sturdy yet balanced starting block for the golf swing.

To practice proper posture, think of being almost in a semi-sitting position. Hold a club lengthways across the back of your shoulders. Lean forward from your upper body only, then flex your knees, making sure that you're still comfortable for the swing.

Your upper body should be still

OVERBENDING YOUR KNEES
Bending your knees too much makes you crouch over the ball. Your back is severely bent and you feel extremely uncomfortable.

NO SHOULDER TURN
As you've bent over so far, you lift rather than swing the club, pointing it left of target. You make very little shoulder turn, giving you no chance of a complete backswing.

reasonably upright and straight – be careful not to stoop as it gives you no chance of swinging to your potential.

Your weight should be spread evenly and your lower legs should feel lively – as if they have springs in them.

When you lower your head to look at the ground, bend your neck – not your shoulders. If your shoulders are too far forward, you're in danger of crouching, which ruins your chances of making a full turn.

ARM POSITION

Once you feel happy in the correct position, take the club from behind your shoulders and grip normally.

Your arms form a V shape, with the left arm hanging straight while the right is a little bent at the elbow – which helps keep away pre-swing stiffness and tension.

Check that your elbows are in a good position by making sure that they point at their respective hip-bones. Try to let your arms and the club form one unit throughout the swing.

STAY RELAXED

Now that you're in position and ready to swing it's vital to remain calm and comfortable so you maintain good posture.

Every moving part of your body must be poised and ready for action – otherwise your swing becomes labored and stilted.

Keep your feet, knees and shoulders lively by making little movements and waggling the club a few times.

This process tunes you up for your swing – as well as keeping you relaxed in the correct, comfortable posture you need to make a full swing.

Check the span
Make sure you are holding the club the proper distance from your body by spanning your right hand from the top of the shaft to your left thigh. If it reaches comfortably – so that you don't have to stretch or bunch your fingers – you're spot on.

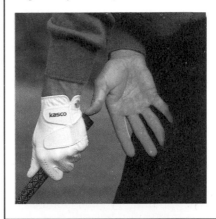

LOCKED KNEES
Straight and stiff legs at address make you lean forward too much as you address the ball. Your body has no chance of fluid movement.

BAD BALANCE AND TURN
It proves impossible to rotate your hips and shoulders to their full extent. Adequate weight transfer and balance become very difficult.

pro tip

Sit on a shooting stick
Imagine you're sitting on a shooting stick. This encourages you to bend your knees from the thighs down. As your knees bend, your back should stay quite straight with your body still upright. Don't use your hips when flexing your knees.

Watch your feet position
Locked knees and toes pointing inwards (left) restrict leg movement. Too much tension in your lower body stops you

making a positive swing. Stand with your feet the same distance apart as your shoulders and point your toes out (right) to promote strong hip turn.

PRACTICE YOUR POSTURE

KEEP A STRAIGHT BACK
To practice the almost semi-sitting position – and reasonably straight back – you need for perfect posture, hold a club lengthways across the back of your shoulders. Lean forward with your upper body only and then flex your knees from the thighs down.

SPREAD YOUR WEIGHT
Make sure your neck – not your shoulders – is bent over and that your weight is evenly spread. Then turn a full 90° – there will be tension in your legs. Turn back and through, so your body twists as far left as it can go.

Seeing the Shot

Everyone makes mental pictures in day-to-day life. Whether you are driving a car, eating or walking, the process of seeing in your mind what needs to be done and activating the required muscles in the body becomes automatic. Achieving the same process in golf lowers your tension – and your score.

One of the advantages of golf is that you have time to prepare for playing the shot. Learn to profit from this by seeing and feeling every shot in your mind and body before you play it. Clear vision beforehand promotes confidence in your ability to play from difficult, as well as easy, lies.

POSITIVE APPROACH

Seeing and feeling your shot brings mind and body together. First you imagine how the ball will fly through the air to the target, including any roll when the ball lands. Then you transfer that picture in your mind into a feeling the body can understand – and produce the correct movement to hit the desired shot.

All great players visualize before hitting a shot. They carefully negotiate every situation within mind and body before making any attempt to play the ball. They know that the concentration needed for golf is different from many other sports.

As golf is a stationary ball game, one of your problems is to stay relaxed and composed at address. This is essential if you are to produce the desired flowing movement in your swing.

Golf requires a relaxed yet positive approach. By making your muscle movement automatic you can stay in an absorbed frame of

PAINT A MENTAL PICTURE
Preparing correctly to play a shot means painting a picture of the ball's path in your mind. Simply imagine the flight of the ball through the air and its roll on landing, allowing for wind and terrain. Leave out of your picture any hazards such as bunkers that are positioned between you and your intended target.

mind and concentrate on making a successful shot.

MUSCLE MEMORY

Before you take your stance, create in your mind a clear picture of

precisely how you want the ball to travel through the air and roll on landing. Remember that factors such as wind, ground conditions and how you feel on the day affect every stroke.

Rub out negative factors such

Concentrate on where you want your shot to pitch, and where you want it to finish.

Steer clear of the ditch, tree and bunker by erasing them from your mind.

Before you step up to the ball, think positively about your shot.

MAKE IT PHYSICAL
With the image of the ball's flight in your mind, transfer the picture into the physical movement required to make your swing. Take a few practice swings as if you are playing the shot itself. Try to achieve muscle memory even when on the practice tee until it becomes an automatic and positive aspect of your game.

as hazards between you and the target. They cause nervousness and uncertainty, which destroy an otherwise good swing.

When you have a crystal-clear mental image, you need to transfer it to a feeling within your body. Do it by taking two or three practice swings that imitate the action you'll use to hit the desired shot.

This routine teaches your body muscle memory. You give it a thorough rehearsal of the shot so that the muscles are not taken by surprise when it matters. You swing smoothly and naturally – your mind is free to concentrate on positive thoughts while your swing takes care of itself.

REGULAR PRACTICE

Now you can address the ball and play the shot by repeating the feeling of your practice swings.

Most of the top players go through this routine on the practice tee as well as on the course. Regular practice is the best way to improve mental pictures of your golf shots. In time, positive thought and feeling become as automatic as other activities of everyday life.

Shut your eyes
Next time you're on the practice tee, try this exercise to develop your skill at seeing the shot, feeling the swing and hitting the ball.

Align yourself to a short target. Close your eyes and imagine the flight of the ball and the swing you need to produce the given shot. After a few practice swings, hit the ball – keeping your eyes shut.

Repeat this several times to increase your feeling for the type of shot required. Once you have mastered the shorter shot, go through the same exercise with longer shots.

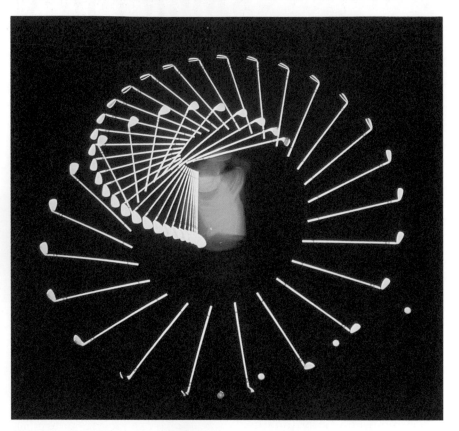

masterclass

Seve's second sight
The greatest visualizer in the modern game is Severiano Ballesteros. As a youngster he had only a 3 iron to practice with. He was forced to use his imagination to create shots not meant for that club, so it required a fine ability to see and feel the shot.

Before playing any stroke, the Spaniard pictures exactly how the ball will travel, sometimes miming the swing without a club. If he is playing from just off the green, he picks the exact spot where the ball should land.

Even today, Ballesteros sometimes plays an entire practice round with one club. It shows the importance he attaches to seeing the shot.

Curing Tension with Nicklaus

Mental tension on the golf course leads to physical tension – and tense muscles mean that you feel clumsy and awkward and your score suffers.

Tension at address can be avoided if you learn a simple pre-shot routine which keeps all parts of your body relaxed, on the move and ready to go. Then you can start your swing smoothly and comfortably by keeping your body moving as you prepare for the shot.

Jack Nicklaus, one of the greatest golfers, has built such a system into his game. He is famous for his precise and methodical approach to every shot. Nicklaus' pre-shot routine has helped him to stay that little bit cooler than his rivals under pressure.

THE TWO C'S

As he stands on the tee, Nicklaus remembers two c's: confidence

NICKLAUS' PRE-SWING
The way to cure mental and physical tension as you stand to the ball is to develop a repeatable pre-shot routine for every stroke. Jack Nicklaus stays absorbed by going through the same movements every time and keeping all the important parts of his body moving.

Soft forearms mean a relaxed grip. Slightly firming up his grip, while making sure it stays soft, is Jack's swing trigger.

The waggle reduces tension because it keeps your body moving. It also boosts muscle memory and helps you to see the shot.

Alternatively moving your feet lightly up and down relaxes your legs. This helps to keep you mobile and ready to swing smoothly.

and concentration.

Confidence comes from being able to repeat successful shots in tough situations – and for that you need experience and practice.

Use self-discipline to make yourself concentrate by going through the same movements before you play each shot.

REPEAT YOUR ROUTINE

Always run through your pre-shot checkpoints: set-up, correct club-

INTERLOCKING GRIP

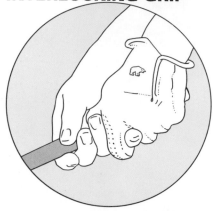

Jack uses the interlocking grip, which is helpful if you have small hands. It is rare among the top players, who use the standard grip.

face aim and body alignment. Jack always checks aim by selecting a marker (a leaf or patch of grass) a few paces in front of his ball directly along the ball-to-target line.

Aim and alignment take time. Jack releases tension by keeping his body moving all the time in the address position. His feet move lightly up and down, in time with gentle swinging back and forth of the club.

This swinging of the club – known as the "waggle" – serves as the preparation for the shot. Nicklaus waggles the club along the line he intends to start the backswing. His waggle is different for every shot: it varies for a fade, a draw or a conventional straight shot.

STAY SOFT

Tension before starting your backswing leads to one particular path of destruction – gripping too tightly. It's impossible to swing smoothly with too firm a grip – it causes a jerky takeaway.

As you stand at address, check that your forearms are "soft" – if your forearms feel supple, you have the correct relaxed grip pressure. Rigid forearms always mean

your grip is too tight.

All that remains in this simple, repeatable procedure is to trigger the swing. Jack uses the "stationary press" – firming up his grip by pressing his hands together a couple of times and relaxing them. It puts his muscles on "action stations," without making them tense. Copy it to give you an effective ignition for a smooth swing.

> ### *Clubhead off the ground*
> Jack Nicklaus does not ground the club at address. He says the habit started at Scioto, the club where he learned to play. The ball used to sit up in the fescue grass rough on the course, and grounding the club sometimes made the ball roll. Young Jack was always concerned about getting a stroke penalty for moving the ball – so he started to hold the club off the ground.
>
> It has other advantages, too. First, lifting the clubhead and waggling it lessens tension. Second, nothing can impede a smooth takeaway. Third, there is no danger of rule-breaking by grounding the club in a bunker.

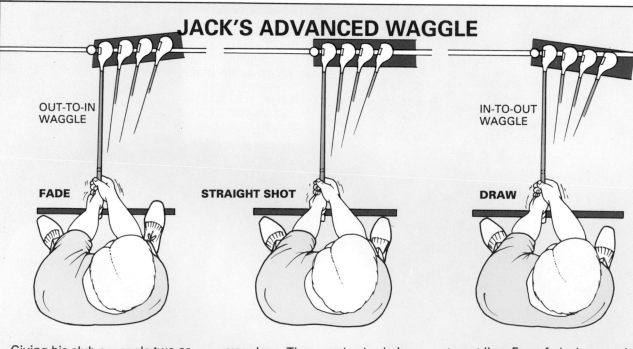

JACK'S ADVANCED WAGGLE

OUT-TO-IN WAGGLE

IN-TO-OUT WAGGLE

FADE

STRAIGHT SHOT

DRAW

Giving his club a waggle two or three times keeps Jack loose before he starts his backswing.

To waggle effectively, include the "moving parts" of your body that you use in the backswing. Moving your feet lightly up and down sends a feeling of mobility to

your legs. The waggle also helps your arms to stay loose and comfortable.

Nicklaus is always careful to waggle along the line he wants to start the backswing. On a normal straight shot, he waggles back and through along the ball-to-

target line. For a fade, he waggles the club on an out-to-in path. If he wants to draw the shot, the path of the waggle is in to out.

This process enhances his confidence, muscle memory and visualization.

Swing with your Body

A complete body action brings together the relevant parts of the golf swing to give you greater consistency. Your shoulders, arms and body move in one piece to help you groove a repeatable swing into your game.

When different parts of your body move independently there's a risk of faults creeping in. A loose, wristy action may give you the occasional good result in a relaxed game. But without precision timing you're bound to lack consistency. A loose swing can desert you completely when the pressure is on.

Nick Faldo is the greatest exponent of the swing with the body. Next time you have a chance to watch him – perhaps when a tournament is televised – notice how

ENHANCE CONTROL
Playing within yourself is one of the keys to consistent golf – most poor shots result from trying to do too much. The swing with your body builds in control. A towel under the arms keeps the swing compact and prevents you from overswinging or trying to hit the ball too hard. With the towel in place, shoot practice balls to a precise spot about 140yd (128m) away.

SWING WITH BODY PRACTICE DRILL

(1) NORMAL AT ADDRESS
Hit shots with a towel held securely under your arms to help you swing with the body – your objective is to keep the towel in place throughout. Adopt your normal address position using no more than a 7 iron.

(2) SLOWLY BACK
Swing smoothly away from the ball keeping your arms close to your body. Let the left arm dominate to encourage a full shoulder turn. Keep the right elbow close to your side to stop the arms moving on an upright plane.

③ THREE-QUARTER BACKSWING
Stop the backswing well short of horizontal –
remember the emphasis is on control and accuracy.
Make sure you complete a full shoulder turn to place
the club on the correct plane. The body is nicely coiled
behind the ball.

④ WEIGHT SHIFT
Start transferring your weight on to the left side
as you begin the downswing. Keep your arms close to
your body to lead the clubhead down to the ball from
inside the line. This arm action also prevents the towel
from slipping.

FOLLOWTHROUGH PRACTICE

⑤ HANDS RELEASE
The left side provides support as the clubhead travels from in to in through impact. The hands release and your arms pull your body around to face the target – the movement through the ball is effortless.

⑥ COMPACT FOLLOWTHROUGH
The followthrough position is compact and tidy, with perfect control from start to finish. Vary your practice routine to gain maximum benefit – hit five shots holding the towel in place and five without the towel.

pro tip

ARMS AND UPPER BODY MOVE TOGETHER

Belt help

Improvise with the belt from your pants to help you groove your swing on the practice tee. You need the help of a friend to fasten the belt correctly – it should fit snugly round your upper arms just above the elbow at address.

Turn your shoulder as you do on a full shot and notice how your arms are held close to the body. This is one of the fundamentals of the swing with your body – it encourages you to swing on a flatter plane for consistency.

HARNESS YOUR SWING

A strap designed by the famous teaching professional David Leadbetter is an effective aid to help you swing with the body.

The strap links your arms and upper body at address and keeps them connected throughout the swing. With regular practice you gradually build the correct moves into your swing.

The strap is on sale in some pro shops. According to the rules of golf it's an artificial aid – you can use it only in practice and never in a competitive round.

rhythmical and compact the swing is, and how fluent his action – no single part of the body moves out of time with another.

Remember, control is the essence of a swing with your body. Never sacrifice accuracy to strive for distance – always swing the club at a tempo that allows you to feel in charge of the clubhead throughout the stroke. Think minimum effort and maximum control.

ONE PIECE TAKEAWAY

The first part of the swing is with your shoulders, arms and club moving smoothly as one away from the ball. Everything moves together to increase your chances of starting the swing on the correct plane.

The coiling of your upper body naturally pulls the left knee in toward the ball – this allows your hips to turn along with the rest of

your body. Your backswing should feel compact but not tense – your right elbow remains close to your side.

If you pick the club up too quickly on the backswing and don't turn properly, the clubhead is thrown in all directions. This excessive wrist movement involves a great deal of guesswork – you trust luck more than judgement to place the club in the correct position.

FULL SHOULDER TURN

A one piece takeaway helps you to swing the club on a wide arc and so achieve a full shoulder turn. These moves place the club on the correct plane at the top of your backswing.

A good swing with your body pulls you into a coiled position behind the ball. Your weight is supported on the right side and your upper back faces the target at the top of the backswing.

If you don't turn properly on the backswing all sorts of problems arise. Your swing plane becomes very upright and easily drifts towards an out-to-in path. You suffer the frustration of cutting across the ball and lose distance on your shots.

It's important to maintain control of the clubhead at the top of the backswing – you don't want to ruin the good work achieved earlier in the swing by making a poor downswing.

SMOOTHLY DOWN

The movement down towards the ball is in one piece, with your shoulders, arms and lower body working in harmony. Shift your weight smoothly to the left.

As the body unwinds on the downswing your hands release the clubhead through impact with tremendous speed. The wide arc of your swing generates the power – no longer should you feel the need for a huge lunge at the ball, which upsets your rhythm and timing.

Almost immediately your striking of the ball benefits from an improvement in consistency. Your poor shots are less wild and far less frequent.

ONE PIECE PUTT
Improve your putting stroke by practicing a shorter version of the swing with your body. Place a club under your arms and adopt your normal putting stance.

Swing the putter smoothly back and through keeping the wrists firm. The triangle shape formed by your arms and shoulders should remain constant. The club under your arms points parallel to the ball-to-target line throughout the stroke.

✗   FLYING ELBOW
If a towel falls from under your right elbow before you complete the backswing, look carefully at the movement of your arms away from the ball.

A flying right elbow is caused by picking the club up too quickly and moving outside the line on the backswing. Your swing then lacks the necessary width and power – this fault usually results in a sliced shot.

✓   KEEP IT COMPACT
Swing the club smoothly away from the ball, moving your arms and upper body in one piece – concentrate on making a full shoulder turn.

Your right arm folds during the backswing and the elbow points straight down. This solid, compact position puts you on the correct plane at the top of the backswing.

Swing checklist
○ Remember, a good backswing places the club on the correct plane at the top and makes it easier to swing down towards the ball correctly. Think of your arms and the club swinging together away from the ball – if you keep the parts moving in one piece you can concentrate on one thought alone.

○ The practice tee is the best place to attempt the swing with your body, so make constructive use of your time there. Swing smoothly and always work on your rhythm. If you swing quickly there's very little time to think what you're doing and it's hard to identify faults.

○ When you practice the swing with your body try to stay relaxed, both at address and during the swing. Often when you introduce new moves into your game the tendency is to tense up. But a rigid swing prevents you gaining benefit from the change.

Improve your Backswing

Astrong backswing makes a great difference to a player's game. The aim is to get the club-head and your hands, arms and body positioned so that you easily and powerfully return the club-face square to the ball.

It's vital to set up the backswing properly – errors at this first stage of the swing are difficult to put right later on.

Before you make a swing, check the basics. Make sure that grip and ball position are correct. With a relaxed posture, align your feet, knees, hips, chest and shoulders parallel to the ball-to-target line.

Although the swing plane and swing path differ from club to club, the technique remains the same. Your posture varies depending on the length of the shaft, but in all cases your knees must be flexed and your back slightly bent. If your back is either too upright or too hunched, or your legs are locked

THE TOP POINT
At the top of the backswing the clubface must be positioned so you can easily return it square to the ball. To achieve this, from address your upper body rotates halfway – about 90° – and your hips, thighs and knees make a quarter turn of 45°. With a full swing, using a wood or long iron, the shaft of the club points at the target – and is parallel to the ball-to-target line.

PERFECT YOUR BACKSWING

①BE RELAXED
At address you should feel relaxed. Your posture must be correct for your body to rotate fully. Your knees are flexed and your back is slightly bent. Your feet should be about the same distance apart as your shoulders.

②KEEP CLUBHEAD LOW
With your hands and arms, take the clubhead away, keeping it low to the ground for the first 1ft (30cm). From here allow your body to rotate to the right. This moves the clubhead inside the ball-to-target line. The clubhead feels closed.

straight, it is impossible to make a full body turn.

Get these basics right and you should make a perfect backswing.

SMOOTH AND SLOW TAKEAWAY

It's vital that you set the right tone for the swing by staying smooth and relaxed

The backswing starts with a unified takeaway, as your hands, arms, shoulders, chest and hips move together.

For the first 1ft (30cm) the clubhead stays close to the ground. From here, the backswing is shaped by your left side – the left shoulder and hip start to rotate to the right (vice versa if you're left handed). This pulls your arms and hands in the same direction and the clubhead moves back and inside the ball-to-target line.

Your left knee moves to the right to allow your hips and shoulders to rotate further. Let your upper body move as one.

From an even distribution at address, your weight then moves on to the inside of your right foot.

MID POINT

Your body continues to rotate to the left and by the mid point on the backswing your right arm starts to fold.

Let your left arm remain comfortably straight but not locked. If you've rotated correctly, by the mid point your left hand, left wrist, left arm and left shoulder should

be joined by an imaginary straight line.

As you rotate further your weight continues to move on to your right side and your right hip feels most of the pressure. But don't let your weight transfer to the outside of your right foot or you'll lose balance.

The more supple you are, the

Mini-club check
Use a mini-club about 2ft (60cm) long to check your position at the top of the backswing. When you look over your right shoulder you can easily see the clubhead of a short-shafted club – which you can't with a normal club. If you have an old club ask your local pro to cut it down for you.

Holding the mini-club with the standard grip, take up the posture and address position for a medium iron. Make a backswing; hold your position at the top.

Your position is correct if the shaft points at the target and the back of your left hand is set at the same angle as the clubface.

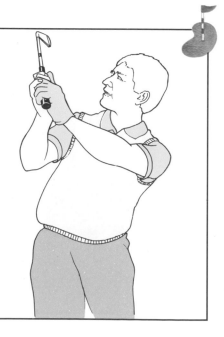

③ MID POINT
By mid point on the backswing your right arm starts to bend. This opens the clubface. Your rotating left shoulder has pulled your left hip to the right. Your weight moves on to your right foot and the toe of the clubhead points at the sky.

④ MOVE SMOOTHLY
As your upper body continues to rotate, your wrists set – they remain in this position to the top of the backswing. Your left knee moves towards the ball and your weight is now on the inside of your right foot. Let your head move with your body.

⑤ CLUBHEAD SWINGS HIGH
At the three-quarter point in the backswing, your rotating shoulders, arms and hands have lifted the clubhead well above your head. Your left arm is still reasonably straight while your right arm is bent. Your legs stay flexed.

⑥ COILED BODY AT TOP
At the top of the backswing your upper body is fully coiled ready to unleash a powerful downswing. Your left arm provides the leverage for pulling the clubhead through the ball. Your upper body has turned about 90° and your hips and knees about 45°.

BE STRAIGHT AT THE TOP

INCORRECT CUPPED POSITION
If your shoulders fail to rotate correctly, and your arms, wrists and hands do not extend fully, the imaginary line is cupped and you slice the shot.

STRAIGHT LINE POSITION (CORRECT)
At the top of the backswing your left arm, left wrist and left hand are joined by an imaginary straight line.

more your head moves naturally as your body rotates. This is fine as long as you keep your eye on the ball.

Your right knee is flexed but not locked, and your lower body supports your upper body as it rotates to the top of the backswing.

TOP OF BACKSWING

By the top of the backswing your upper body has rotated halfway around – about 90° – while your hips, thighs and knees have made a quarter turn – about 45°. Your right arm is considerably bent while your left arm remains reasonably straight.

This is important. If your left arm is either crooked or limp you lose power on the downswing. A straight left arm provides a powerful lever for pulling the clubhead through the ball.

At the top of a good backswing your body feels coiled and ready to unwind, unleashing power on the downswing.

The exact positioning varies depending on the length of the shaft. Although your upper body must always rotate about 90°, the length of your swing alters. You should make a full swing with a wood and a long iron, but only a three-quarter swing with a medium and short iron.

The back of your left wrist and left hand and the clubface are set at the same angle. With a medium iron you make a three-quarter swing – though your upper body still turns 90°.

Allow for a very slight pause at the top of the backswing before starting the downswing. Although this pause shouldn't be long enough to be visible, it lets your body change direction smoothly. A pause also prevents you from rushing the start of the downswing.

RELAX AT ADDRESS

You can't rotate correctly if you're tense at address. Tension can affect most parts of your body. It makes your muscles tighten, which restricts body movement and stops your chest, shoulders and arms from rotating fully.

There are a number of ways to relieve tension. One is to do a few warm-up or stretching exercises before picking up a club. Another is to lift the clubhead just off the ground and waggle your feet at address. This keeps your muscles ticking over and stops them from becoming stiff.

If you still find it difficult to make a full swing, even after a warm-up session, don't try to force one. Not only can this cause injury, it also affects your tempo. Providing your body rotates correctly and you keep your rhythm, a three-quarter backswing is enough until you are able to develop a full swing.

INCORRECT ARCHED POSITION
If the clubhead moves too far inside the ball-to-target line on the backswing, the imaginary line is arched and you produce a hook.

pro tip

Your flat right hand
Using a driver, the palm of your right hand should be flat enough at the top of the backswing to support a few books. Check this by holding your position at the top. Remove the club with your left hand. Is the right palm flat?

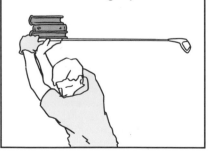

Improve your Downswing

The aim of the downswing is to return the clubface square to the ball with as much power as you can deliver – you need good tempo and rhythm to maintain the flow.

The downswing is the most complex movement to learn and perfect. You are usually taught the backswing and downswing as two separate parts, but in fact the downswing begins before the backswing has ended. They must now be put together to form one fluent movement.

Your backswing prepares you to strike the ball. In completing it, the upper body coils 90° while the lower body turns only 45°. The lower body becomes the trigger for your downswing. Your weight has shifted to your right hip pocket area and you should be in a relaxed and powerful position.

THE TRIGGER

The key to making a good downswing is to link your legs to your arms correctly. Your chest, arms, wrists and hands must move together.

If you raise your left heel during the backswing, the downswing begins by you firmly planting it back on the ground. This action triggers the left hip and starts a weight shift back to the left side.

If you are young and supple you don't need to lift your left heel to complete the backswing. The left hip now starts the downswing, pulling the hands, arms and club down to the mid point position.

POWER AND ACCURACY

This movement automatically drops the club on a path slightly inside that of your backswing. Any sudden or awkward move at this

STARTING THE DOWNSWING

The downswing begins before the backswing has ended – your hips start to move back to the ball before you reach the top point.

YOUR HEAD
Although your left eye should be looking down on the back of the ball, your head has turned slightly to the right.

UPPER BODY
Turn your chest so that your back faces the target. Your upper body rotates 90° from the address position.

LEGS AND LOWER BODY
Your legs are flexed and ready to provide power through the ball. They turn only 45°.

PERFECTING THE DOWNSWING

Turn into impact

To imitate the position your body should be in at impact, adopt your normal address position with your hands and arms stretched out. Concentrate on turning your left hip to the left which twists your middle body towards the target. Do this slowly four or five times so you can see how correct hip rotation returns the arms to impact.

① **THE TOP**
At the top point you should feel poised and ready for action. Your upper body coils 90° while your hips turn 45° and provide stability for your swing. Feel your weight transfer to your right hip pocket. The right knee remains flexed to let the legs support the upper body. The shaft of the club should point parallel to your ball-to-target line.

② **FIRST MOVEMENT**
Turn your left hip smoothly to the left. This triggers the weight shift back to your left side. Feel your left hip linked to your left hand and arm – they all move together and must not separate. As the left hip starts the downswing, the hands and arms automatically drop inside the path of the backswing. This natural movement starts before you've completed the backswing.

(3) **MID POINT**
The hands and arms respond to the movement of your lower body. The hips continue to lower the hands and arms toward the ball. This is where you should feel immensely powerful. But don't attempt to hit the ball at this stage – your power is stored in your wrists, which must not unhinge too early in the swing.

(4) **READY FOR IMPACT**
As you continue to turn the left hip to the left, the clubhead returns back to the ball and is naturally square at impact. Using your hips and legs correctly means no conscious hand action is necessary.

point is disastrous. At the mid point, your left arm acts as a powerful lever, pulling the clubhead into the ball and storing power.

Your hands and arms are responding to the movement of your lower body. As the left hip continues turning to the left the hands and arms deliver the clubhead back to the ball with power and accuracy.

WEIGHT TRANSFER

During the downswing your weight transfers from your right side to your left – by impact slightly more than half your weight is on the inside of your left foot. Your head stays still until you strike the ball.

You must feel the downswing with your feet. They help generate power and coordinate the entire swing. If the hip and leg action is incorrect you lose all smoothness. Correct hip rotation allows your arms, wrists and hands to remain passive.

If your lower body doesn't rotate correctly on the downswing, your hands, wrists and arms shape the swing path. The clubhead moves outside the ball-to-target line at the start of the downswing before being pulled across your body from out to in. At impact the clubface isn't square and you slice the ball.

CORRECT YOUR STARTING POSITION

If the club is in the wrong position at the start of the downswing it is difficult to return the clubface square to the ball. The shaft of the club should point at the target. If the shaft points left of the target (above left) you swing through impact from out to in, producing a slice. If it points right of the flag (above right) you swing from in to out, creating a hook. Most poor positions are caused by incorrect upper body rotation.

pro tip

Better body turn

To develop correct body rotation on the downswing, practice the following routine. Holding the club normally in your left hand, place your right hand mid way down the shaft so that it rests against your open fingers. Reverse the hands if you're left handed. Turn your shoulders and let your arms swing to the top of your backswing. From here feel the left hip pulling the arms down. Do this a few times to understand how your hands, wrists, arms, chest and club are dropped into a position to deliver the clubhead at impact.

Impact

The impact position is the point during the swing when you're about to strike the ball. It's the moment when – if you swing correctly – the clubhead finally catches up with your hands.

To hit a golf ball both long and straight down the fairway, you must return the clubhead to the ball with two qualities – power and accuracy.

Your body position at impact differs for irons and woods, but ball position and shaft length combine to alter the strike. With woods, no divot is taken as you sweep the ball – which is opposite your left heel – off the fairway or tee.

To gain top benefit from an iron club, it's vital to strike the ball first, before taking a small divot. Move the ball towards the center of your stance as the shaft length shortens.

SQUARE CLUBFACE

There are many different types of correct golf swing – but only one correct impact position. This means returning the clubface squarely to the ball, which leads to straight hitting. Building power is more complicated.

You coil power in the backswing – this power is stored at the top. As your downswing begins, your lower body starts a weight shift to the left and your shoulders, arms and hands follow, before finally releasing the clubhead at impact.

Being in the proper impact

ONE IMPACT POSITION
Although there are many types of golf swing, there is only one impact position. It's similar to the set-up – the clubface is square to the ball, but the lower body is shifting left.

INCORRECT: NO LOWER BODY MOVEMENT

CLUB STAYS AHEAD

Starting your swing with your shoulders and failing to move your lower body left means that most of your weight stays firmly fixed on the right. You swing the clubface across the line, which closes the clubface and causes a slice.

WRONG: WEIGHT STAYS ON RIGHT

INCORRECT: MOVING AHEAD

EARLY WEIGHT TRANSFER

As you start the downswing, you shift your weight too quickly to the left, and you move ahead of the clubhead. At impact the club has no chance of catching up, usually causing an open clubface – and a push.

WRONG: WEIGHT SHIFTS TOO EARLY

PRACTICE YOUR HAND POSITION

① ADDRESS
Stand with knees flexed in your normal address position. Hold out both arms in front of you, as if about to take grip.

② TOP OF BACKSWING
Leave your left arm straight and swing your right arm to the top of the backswing position. Slowly move your hips back to the left, keeping your knees bent.

③ IMPACT
Look at your hand positions. They should have returned to impact solely through lower body movement. No conscious hand action should be needed.

CORRECT WEIGHT SHIFT THROUGH IMPACT

CLUBHEAD CATCHES UP WITH HANDS
As you start your downswing, your left hip turns to the left – enough to transfer your weight to your left foot. This movement lowers your hands and arms to the mid point position. You should feel very powerful, with both arms loaded with energy. The muscles in your left hip

and thigh keep turning smoothly to the left and your right leg and knee follow. Your lower body is taut but springy. The shot does not finish with the strike – your weight continues to your left side, letting your upper body turn and face the target. This movement brings your head up to watch the ball's flight.

pro tip

USE AN UMBRELLA

Drive an umbrella into the ground and set up as normal with the outside of your left foot (right foot for left-handers) touching the umbrella. Make your usual swing.

You're in the correct position at impact if your left knee touches the umbrella, but the space remains between your hip and the umbrella.

position ensures that you achieve maximum distance and the correct trajectory. If you're out of position, you're likely to hit fat (behind the ball) or thin (halfway up).

HIP ACTION

To hit squarely at impact, you must start the downswing with the correct hip action by turning your hips smoothly left.

Feel as if your hips pull the arms and hands down until the mid point of the downswing, when your arms should be loaded with power. Your shoulders send power to your arms, the arms to the hands and your hands pass it on to the clubhead.

If everything else is as it should be, the clubface is square on contact. Don't try to control the clubface at this point – it's moving far too quickly.

At impact, the clubhead, arms and hands form a straight line, although your position is not identical to the one you adopt at setup. This is because your lower body carries on turning to the left, so that your weight shifts fully from your right side. Keep your head steady.

Remember that you haven't finished playing the shot when you strike the ball – it's important to make a full followthrough.

Improve your Followthrough

Your followthrough – sometimes called the through-swing – is vital to your swing. You must swing through to a good finish on all your shots – this promotes accuracy and power and helps you keep smooth rhythm and tempo.

Unfortunately many golfers concentrate so hard on hitting the ball that they forget about achieving a correct followthrough. They quit on the ball and lose power and distance. Your swing does not finish when you hit the ball – the golf swing is complete when your body turns around to a balanced finish after impact.

The finish provides a good guide to the rest of your swing as it confirms the movements you have made before. Look for clues

COMPLETE YOUR SWING

A solid followthrough is an essential part of the complete golf swing. A repeatable swing is your goal so to perfect your movements you must assume the key positions consistently.

HEAD FORCED UP
Your head is forced up as your right shoulder comes around. This lets your arms swing the club around your body to the finish.

WEIGHT TRANSFER
After impact your body must keep turning – and your weight should transfer – to the left. As this happens your right shoulder swivels in the same direction.

CLUBHEAD SPEED
At a point just after impact the clubhead reaches top speed. It is this speed – with proper weight transfer – that carries you through to the followthrough position.

BALANCE
You finish steady on your feet – most of the weight is on the outside of your left foot, with your right foot almost vertical.

Trouble both sides
When you're playing a tough hole with trouble on both sides, your confidence is likely to waver – just when you need it most.

Lack of confidence in the throughswing causes you to quit on the shot after impact. Without a proper throughswing your strike is stifled and balance impaired. You need to know that you can rely on repeating your finish position, so that you play a powerful – and straight – stroke, even under pressure.

Concentrate on your followthrough – that's when the shot finishes, not when you hit the ball. Thinking about your finish helps take your mind off any pressure – and off impact – so that you focus on rhythm throughout your swing.

in your followthrough to diagnose swing faults.

REVERSE THE BACKSWING

Most players realize that good body turn is vital during the backswing – but forget that they need to repeat this on the followthrough.

To help build your throughswing, you can reverse an exercise you tried when you were developing the backswing.

Set yourself into your final followthrough position and rewind your body, arms and club until you come back to the impact position. This helps you to find the correct throughswing plane – it should feel like your backswing reversed.

It's unlikely that you'll achieve a valid followthrough unless your top of the backswing position is good.

Tempo is vital – it gives each part of your body the time to respond correctly and evenly during the swing. Smooth rhythm leads to a regular, clean strike as the moving parts of your body slot into the proper places. You must have fluid movement from the top of the backswing to the end of the throughswing to promote this tempo either side of impact.

WEIGHT TRANSFER

A good followthrough needs sound weight transfer. From the top of the backswing – when most of your weight is on the right foot – you shift your weight to the left. In your finish position you should be balanced with most of your weight on the outside of your left foot.

If you don't shift your weight properly you're likely to stay flat footed as you swing through, and

MAKING A CLASSIC FOLLOWTHROUGH

①INTO IMPACT Your hips lead your shoulders all the way on the downswing as you make a smooth strike through the ball. At impact you're just beginning to lift your right heel up.

②FLUID MOVEMENT Keep your movements smooth after you strike – just because you've hit the ball, it doesn't mean that you've finished playing the shot. Your head remains still.

A MATTER OF BALANCE

✓ A sound throughswing means that you're steady, with most weight on the outside of your left foot. The ball gains good distance.

✗ If your weight fails to shift from right to left on the downswing, you're left flat footed. In most cases this leads to a slice.

✗ Throwing your lower body weight too much right to left on the downswing leaves you likely to overbalance forward. It usually causes a push.

③ **HEAD COMES AROUND**
Your upper body continues to clear to the left, so that your turning right shoulder begins to force your head round and up to watch the ball's flight. Most of your weight has shifted to the left side.

④ **SHOULDERS CATCH UP**
Because your head has come around, your upper body clearance is not obstructed, helping you apply maximum power. Your shoulders catch up with your hips at the end of the swing. Your right foot is vertical, resting lightly on the ground.

WHERE ARE YOU FACING?

1 BACKSWING
Use a club to check your position. A good backswing leads to an effective throughswing. At the top of your backswing, your followthrough is reversed – your shoulders are 90° to the ball-to-target line. Your back faces the target and the club is almost horizontal.

2 DOWNSWING
The smooth tempo on your downswing should be the same as on your throughswing – the club must not slow down. By impact, your rotating upper body should be parallel to the ball-to-target line.

3 FOLLOWTHROUGH
Your finish is like the top of the backswing reversed. Your shoulders are 90° to the ball-to-target line, and your chest faces the target.

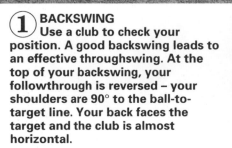

Complete your lower body turn

✗ The lower body must be correct if the upper body is to follow suit. Bringing your legs and hips only part of the way around reduces your chances of making a full, powerful strike.

✓ Your throughswing is fully effective only if your lower body completes its turn, and you end in a balanced position with your weight mainly on the outside of your left foot.

you lose distance. This usually happens because you start the downswing with your hands and arms instead of working from your hips. You don't have time to transfer weight before impact.

Pushing too hard with your lower body also causes erratic weight transfer. You fail to swing around your body, making a balanced finish impossible.

HEAD MOVEMENT

Keeping your head down too long after impact destroys any chance you had of achieving a correct followthrough.

Watch the clubhead strike the ball but then let your right shoulder – which should be turning smoothly left – gently force your head around to face the target. If your head stays down too long it gets in the way of your body's clearing action and prevents a full followthrough.

Tempo and Rhythm

To be a consistent striker of the ball your swing must have good tempo and rhythm. Tempo is the speed at which you swing the club while rhythm is its fluency.

Good tempo and rhythm allow every moving part of your body to coordinate as a single unit. Although your head, shoulders, arms, hands, hips, knees and feet have their own function, they must work together during the swing. If your tempo is too fast or erratic, this doesn't happen and you don't make a solid strike.

Even if your set-up is perfect and you swing the clubhead along the correct path, you only play effective golf when your tempo and rhythm are relaxed and smooth.

DEVELOPING YOUR TEMPO

Most players with poor tempo and rhythm swing the club too fast in a vain attempt to work up power and distance. A quick or rushed swing doesn't allow each individual movement enough time to perform its task and your action is jerky.

To find your natural tempo and rhythm concentrate on swinging the club smoothly. Start with a half swing. Only when you achieve a solid, consistent strike should you lengthen your swing to three-quarter and then full.

Developing your ideal tempo and rhythm takes practice as well as natural ability. Once they improve you can build a repeatable swing.

It is vital you concentrate on keeping a good tempo and rhythm when playing a round. Once

SWINGING SMOOTHLY
Good tempo and rhythm allow each individual movement within your swing to work correctly and help produce a perfect swing path. If your swing is too quick your body hasn't enough time to rotate properly and the clubface isn't square at impact.

UNDERSTANDING TEMPO AND RHYTHM

① **TAKEAWAY**
The takeaway dictates the speed of the swing. If you rush it, the rest of your swing becomes too fast and erratic. Concentrate on taking the club away smoothly.

② **THE BACKSWING**
Your backswing must have a smooth and even rhythm. This allows your hands, arms and shoulders to move as one, and helps you to feel the clubhead throughout the stroke.

③ **TOP OF BACKSWING**
Allow for a slight pause at the top of the backswing to ensure that you complete it. This prevents you from rushing the downswing.

you've selected the club to fit into your game plan, your only thought should be making a smooth swing. Visualize your swing as a whole. Avoid analyzing any specific movement within your swing just as you blot out hazards on the fairway.

RECOVERING LOST TEMPO

No player – even leading professionals – consistently maintains perfect tempo and rhythm. Regaining your timing isn't difficult – as long as you go back to basics.

Once you establish a regular distance with each club, recover lost tempo and rhythm by playing to a shorter target. Reduce the distance you try to send each shot by about one-third. This automatically slows your swing down, allowing each body movement enough time to function.

By slowing down and reducing the length of your swing you

④ **THE DOWNSWING**
The downswing must have the same tempo and swing path as the backswing. To help you swing the club on the same line, the start of the downswing must be smooth.

⑤ **IMPACT**
To make a solid strike your tempo and rhythm must be perfect. Your swing movements must coordinate properly so that the clubface is square at impact.

⑥ **FOLLOWTHROUGH**
Your swing slows down as smoothly as it increased at takeaway. Good tempo and rhythm look effortless and should become natural and consistent with regular practice.

SHORTEN YOUR SWING

  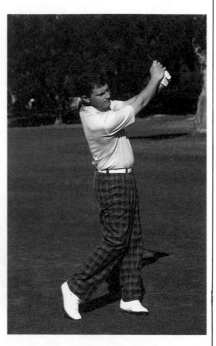

One of the best ways to improve – as well as understand – tempo and rhythm is to practice a three- | **quarter swing. By shortening your swing you slow it down and it is easier for its individual movements** | **to coordinate correctly. A three-quarter swing also increases clubhead feel.**

lessen tension and develop greater clubhead feel. You also hit the ball further than you expect because you achieve a more solid strike.

With a slower action it is easier to identify any faults in your set-up and swing – and then correct them. From here you can increase your tempo until your swing combines rhythm, consistency and power.

FEET TOGETHER

Another exercise for finding good tempo and rhythm is to hit the ball with your feet together. Because your center of gravity is higher than with a normal stance you must reduce the speed, length and power of your swing to avoid losing balance.

The best way to understand and appreciate tempo and rhythm is to watch top players – either at tournaments or on television. Although they all swing the club differently their tempo and rhythm are perfect.

Take an image of their swing on to the practice range or course and try to copy it. It's amazing how you can improve your own swing – and your game – by trying to imitate top players.

REDUCE YOUR DISTANCE

If your swing is too fast, slow it down by reducing the distance you try to hit each shot. For example, if you normally expect to strike a 5 iron about 150yd (136m), go to the practice tee and aim at a target 100yd (91m) away. This makes you reduce the length, speed and power of your normal swing, and helps you develop a smoother action.

Fringe Play

Even top professionals don't hit every green in regulation, so they spend hours practicing the art of fringe play. They fully appreciate that the ability to get up and down in two is just as important as striking the full shots well.

Fringe grass is evenly cut and similar in length to light rough. A chip from the fringe is a short shot – there's seldom more than 30yd (27m) between you and the flag.

Unlike most other shots in golf, there are no obstacles in front of you to worry about.

STROKE SAVERS

There's more than one way to play a chip from the fringe and every one is a potential stroke saver. It's vital that you understand which club is best suited to any given situation, so try not to restrict

CHIP AWAY AT YOUR SCORE
Intelligent club selection and knowing how the ball reacts from different lies are just as important for the short game as a correct technique. A low running chip is a safe shot likely to give you consistent results. Don't lob the ball high into the air from short range unless you have very little green to work with.

CHIP AND RUN OFF FRINGE

1 SQUARE ON
When there's plenty of green between you and the flag the ideal shot is the chip and run. Select a spot on the green where you intend to pitch the ball. The ball is in contact with the ground for most of its journey, so consider the speed and slope of the green – the roll of the ball is influenced by both. Stand square to the target with the ball central in your stance. Keep your hands ahead of the clubhead at address – they should remain that way throughout the swing.

3 NUDGE FORWARD
The left hand leads the clubhead down on a shallow angle of attack into the bottom of the ball. Keep the hands ahead of the clubhead at all times to prevent the dreaded scooping action at impact. Don't worry about getting the ball airborne – the loft of the club does this for you. This is a simple back and through movement with the hands and arms. Don't hit down sharply at the ball – neither height nor backspin are required for this shot.

(2) SLOWLY BACK
Take the club away from the ball smoothly and break the wrists only a little. The length of backswing determines the length of the shot. Feel your left hand in complete control of the club – the right hand acts mainly in a supporting role for a shot as short as this.

(4) BALL RUNS UP TO HOLE
Long after the ball is on its way to the hole your left hand should be held ahead of the clubhead. Concentrate on keeping the clubface pointing at the target. The ball pitches less than halfway to the flag and runs up to the hole. A successful chip leaves you a very makeable putt for your next shot.

HIGH AND SHORT

1. HANDS AHEAD
When the ball sits down in fringe grass and there's very little green to work with, a sand wedge is the club for the job. Adopt an open stance with the ball back in your stance and your hands forward.

2. STEEP BACK
Break the wrists very early in the backswing – the sideways movement of the hands is tiny but the hinge effect of the wrists gives you enough length on the backswing.

yourself to a personal favorite.

Check the lie of the ball, the distance between you and the flag and the ground conditions on the green – these three factors determine the club you should use. Let your imagination work in your favor – select a spot where you want the ball to pitch and visualize it running up towards the hole.

Take a couple of practice swings to develop a feel for the shot you've chosen. These swings help you focus your mind on the task in hand and prevent you rushing in too hastily.

FLOAT SHOT

When the ball sits down in a fluffy lie and there's not much green to work with, you're faced with a difficult chip. But a sound technique and sensible club selection help you out of trouble every time. You need to generate clubhead speed to avoid the duffed shot while at the same time taking care not to overhit the ball.

Reach for your sand wedge and stand open to the ball-to-target line. Lay the clubface open in your stance so that it aims squarely at the flag. Adopt a weak left hand grip to prevent the clubface closing during the swing. Break the wrists quickly on the backswing and cut down across the ball from out to in. Like taking sand with a bunker shot, you rely on the grass acting as a cushion at impact. The ball pops up in the air, lands softly on the green and runs very little.

If you're fortunate enough to find your ball in a good lie, this is altogether a much easier shot. The ball may fly up a little higher – and so run less – but exactly the same techniques apply.

LOW RUNNER

When there's plenty of green between you and the flag, a shot with a lower trajectory is required. If the lie is good use an 8 iron – you want the ball to travel in the air for less than half of its journey to the hole.

Select a spot on the green where you aim to pitch the ball. Gauge the slope of the green – the ball runs along the ground for most of the way and takes any breaks in the same way as a putt. Set up fairly square to the target and position the ball towards the center of your stance.

Swing your arms back and through, keeping the left wrist firm and dominant. The ball is lofted over the fringe on to the putting surface and runs smoothly up towards the hole.

From a poor lie use a more lofted club, perhaps a 9 iron. The techniques which served you well from a good lie help you again in this slightly trickier situation. Address the ball in exactly the same way. Make sure your hands are ahead of the ball – all types of chipping faults can stem from positioning your hands behind the ball.

Swing back with a small amount of wrist break and accelerate the clubhead down into the bottom of the ball. Grass comes between the clubface and the ball, so don't concern yourself with backspin. The ball comes out quite low and runs a long way.

(3) RETURN TO ADDRESS
Grass acts as a cushion at impact – as sand does on a bunker shot – so accelerate on the downswing. The importance of a correct set-up becomes clear as you return to exactly the same position as address

(4) SOFT TOUCH
This is a perfect example of the paradox of hitting down on the ball to gain height on the shot – the natural loft of the club pops the ball up in the air. Your head remains perfectly still throughout.

Rules check

With a putter in your hands it's easy to mark and lift your ball simply out of habit – but you risk breaking the rules if you do so when your ball has come to rest on the fringe.

Most courses allow you this luxury only when winter rules are in force, so check the noticeboard in the clubhouse before you step on to the course. An infringement of this rule costs you a hole in matchplay and 2 penalty shots in strokeplay.

(5) LEFT IN CHARGE
Notice how dominant the left hand is even though the ball is well on its travels – at no time in the shot is the clubhead allowed to overtake the hands. The ball lands softly on the green and runs very little.

CLOSELY CUT

The apron tends to be only a few paces wide and skirts around every green between the fringe and the putting surface. The grass is just slightly longer than you find on the green – for this reason your putter is usually the most effective club. The ball is always in contact with the ground, so you eliminate the risk of an uneven bounce.

If the apron is damp from early morning dew or rain, a shot with a 7 iron using your putting stroke can produce excellent results. Your stance, grip and ball position remain the same as if you were holding a putter. A smooth stroke gently lofts the ball over the apron, preventing any dampness slowing it down.

FRINGE BENEFITS

More than half of your shots in a round of golf are chips and putts, so at least half of your practice should be devoted to this aspect of the game.

You can spend hours practicing your short game and not become in the least bit tired – chipping requires little physical effort.

To make your practice enjoyable vary the type of shot you play. Experiment with different clubs and learn to understand how the ball reacts.

In the winter months you can also practice your putting indoors – and even some gentle chipping with an air ball. With enough practice you are certain to develop into an accomplished chipper of the ball – your scores are bound to tumble as a result.

Reach for an iron
If your ball is nestling down slightly in the fringe grass you can use any club from a 7 iron to a pitching wedge. The club you choose depends on the amount of green you have to work with. A good maxim to remember is less green/more loft, and more green/less loft.

Don't putt
Even if you're close to the flag, rule out any hope of using a putter from this lie – it usually leads to disaster. The straight face of the putter is totally unsuited to playing from the fluffy grass on the fringe. Pace is almost impossible to judge so take a lofted club instead.

APRON PUTTER

Not all putters are suited to apron play. Use one that gives a smooth roll – if the ball jumps into the air on impact it's likely to pull up short.

An **offset** putter lofts the ball slightly at impact – though the ball is briefly in the air it rolls smoothly once on the green.

A **mallet** putter isn't suited to apron play. The ball hops at impact – speed is lost and the putt pulls up short of the hole.

A conventional **blade** putter is ideal. Struck from the sweet spot the ball runs smoothly along the ground towards the hole.

Avoid a **center shafted** putter. The ball jumps into the air and you can't judge pace accurately.

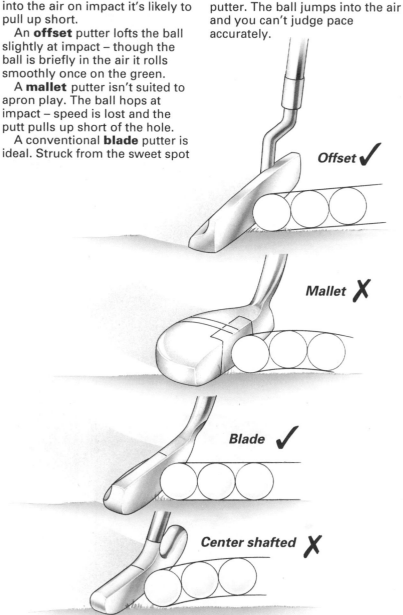

Offset ✓

Mallet ✗

Blade ✓

Center shafted ✗

Sand Wedge around the Green

Balanced downhill stance

Most amateurs use their sand wedge around the green from only a bunker or rough grass. But there is great scope for a variety of shots to be played with the same club. Instead of using clubs from the 7 iron upwards for different situations, it's possible to manufacture every greenside chip shot with a sand wedge.

It's not for everyone, but the advantage of using the same club for nearly every situation is that you can cultivate good feel and touch. By regularly playing the sand wedge you know instinctively how the ball behaves whatever way you use the club. This helps your confidence. Chipping with a different club each time

HAZARDOUS LOB
Because the sand wedge is the most lofted club in the bag it's perfect for delicate lobs. Facing a chip over trouble from a downhill lie, position the ball slightly further back in your stance – to help avoid the thin – and choke down the grip. Try to tilt with the slope and push your weight forward to be sturdy. If the slope is steep, press on the inside of your back foot for balance. Pick the club up quickly with plenty of wrist break (above) to follow the contours of the slope. A steep attack also helps the ball to gain height.

makes judging the shot tricky – shaft length and loft vary with each club.

Playing the sand wedge in most situations also forces you to be creative each time. It helps you to visualize shots effectively, not only around the green but in every department of your game.

CHANGING CHIPS

The various sand wedge shots – perhaps a chip and run or high lob over trouble – are easy to play. Slightly alter your ball position, stance, clubface loft and type of swing.

The **long chip and run** shot is usually associated with a straighter faced club like a 7 or 8 iron but a sand wedge can be used just as effectively. Place the ball well back in the stance and push your hands forward, taking loft off the clubface.

Play the stroke with a firm wristed action – strike down crisply on the ball, and don't quit. The ball flies much lower than a conventional sand wedge, then checks on the second bounce and runs up to the hole.

Use the same technique for the **short chip over a fringe**. Most golfers opt for a putter, but sometimes there's a risk of an irregular roll through the grass and so pace is difficult to judge – especially on fast greens. A little bump off the back foot with a sand wedge lifts the ball just enough to clear the fringe and the ball rolls toward the pin. You may be surprised how often you hole out once you have thoroughly practiced this technique.

The **low running** sand wedge can also replace the 8 iron for a bump and run up a slope to a flag cut just on the green. Instead of pinning trust on the ball bouncing several times up the slope, you can play a sand wedge so that it bounces only once or twice, lessening the risk of the shot taking bad hops. But the sand wedge shot has to be played precisely so practice the stroke before you attempt it on the course.

The one time you should hit another club is when you're faced with a chip off hard, bare ground. The danger of thinning or fluffing the shot outweighs any advantage gained. Reach instead for a straighter faced club.

ONE FOR ALL

BUMP AND RUN
Don't be afraid of using the sand wedge from just off the green instead of a straight faced iron or putter – it's a simple shot to play. Position the ball well back in your stance – opposite the right foot – and push your hands forward to deloft the clubface. Push your weight forward also. With a firm wristed putting action strike down firmly on the ball – it pops up to clear the fringe but flies low enough so that it runs on landing.

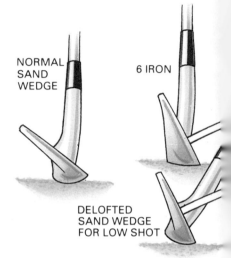

NORMAL SAND WEDGE

6 IRON

DELOFTED SAND WEDGE FOR LOW SHOT

CHECKING CHIP
An 8 iron is a good choice for a chip over a medium sized fringe provided the target is far enough away – the ball rolls on landing. A sand wedge can be played like an 8 iron, but the shot checks more on landing. This gives you extra control but the ball still rolls, which is especially useful on fast greens or going downhill.

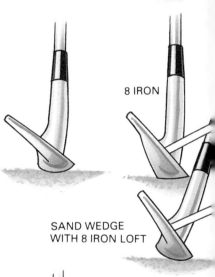

8 IRON

SAND WEDGE WITH 8 IRON LOFT

DELICATE TOUCH
A chip over a large fringe with little green to work with is a perfect situation for the sand wedge. A pitching wedge is fine but needs to be played very precisely for the ball to go close. The sand wedge gains more height and lands softly so you can afford to be slightly bolder. But think again about using the lob with the sand wedge if it has to be played from hard pan. The pitching wedge is then the better option.

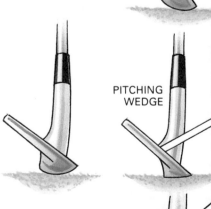

PITCHING WEDGE

SAND WEDGE LANDS SOFTLY

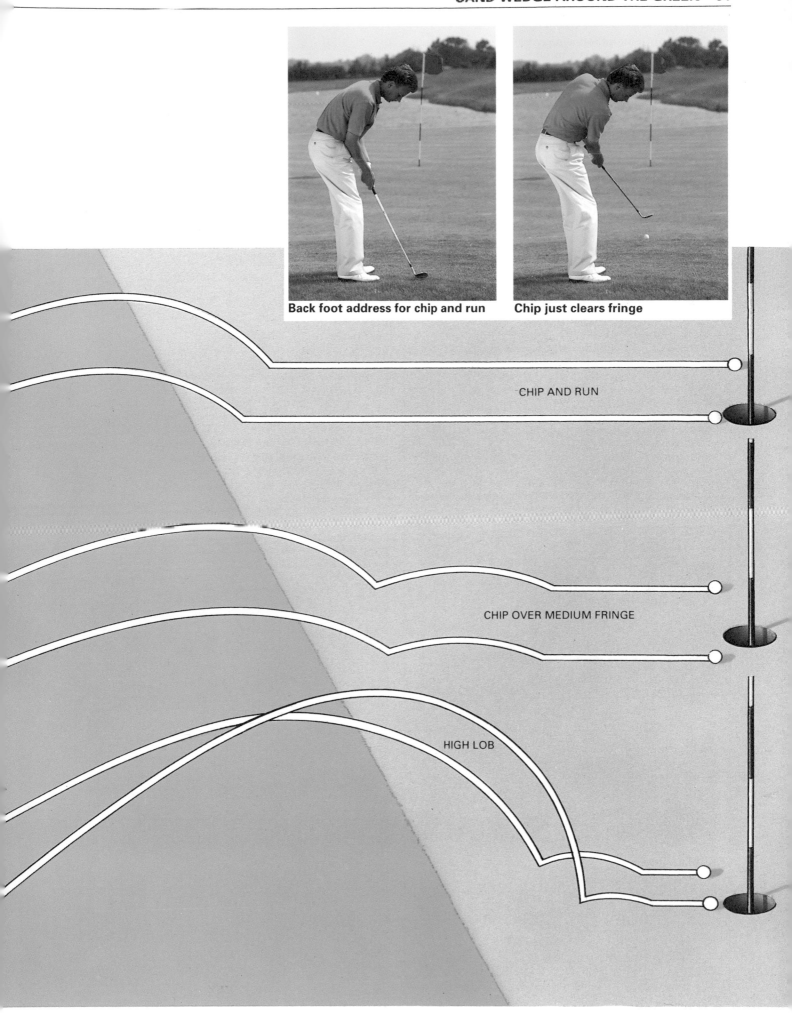

Back foot address for chip and run

Chip just clears fringe

CHIP AND RUN

CHIP OVER MEDIUM FRINGE

HIGH LOB

HIGH PITCH

The high, soft-landing lob is easy to play because the swing is almost full. With the ball forward in your stance, align slightly left allowing the blade to be opened up for extra loft. Your backswing should be steep and wristy but full. The length of your swing determines the distance you hit the ball. Swing down steeply and follow through fully – never flick at the ball or quit on the shot. Don't attempt this stroke off hard bare ground – thinning the ball is all too easy.

Make a steep swing...   ...and full followthrough

McNulty's versatility

Mark McNulty is superb around the green, getting up and down more often than not from any position. His great touch and confidence let him play the sand wedge when most other golfers would hesitate.

Even though the ball is just in the fringe and a putter could be used for the short distance to the flag, Mark opts to bump a sand wedge. The ball jumps just enough to clear the fringe but still rolls like a putt when on the green. This technique is ideal for coping with pacy greens such as those at Valderrama, the 1990 Volvo Masters venue where McNulty finished equal fourth.

pro tip

Sharpen your sand wedge

The feel, control and confidence you gain from playing a sand wedge creatively around a green can be found only by constant practice. An excellent way to develop this touch is to stand in the middle of the practice green and throw a number of balls around it – place them randomly by tossing them over your shoulder.

Without changing any of the lies or positions, work your way around the green playing each ball as you find it. You soon learn how to alter your set-up and swing to cope with every situation.

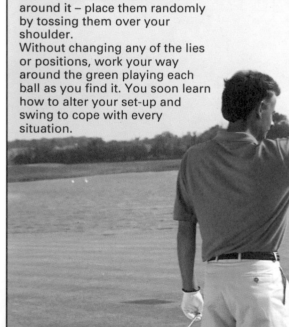

High Cut-up Shot

UP AND OVER
With a rough covered bank between you and the green, a high cut-up pitch is the only shot that gives you a realistic hope of getting up and down in 2. It removes as many elements of chance as you possibly can in golf. Use your sand wedge, stand open to the ball-to-target line and make a smooth, full swing. The clubhead slides through the grass and the ball flies high over the bank. If you judge the shot well, you can expect a soft landing on the green.

pro tip

Take your pick
The key to good scoring is possessing a sharp touch around the greens. It's important to give yourself the best possible chance to excel in this department of your game, because it's the best way to knock strokes off your handicap.

Try carrying four short game clubs in your bag – a 9 iron, a pitching wedge and two sand wedges, one with standard loft and a second utility wedge with a few degrees extra. This range of clubs gives you great versatility around the greens.

Far too many club players' golf bags are heavily biased in favor of the long game. They might carry 3 different woods, plus a 1 and a 2 iron, but this is almost certainly too many long clubs. Analyzed closely, most golfers would probably find they rarely use some of them.

There are a number of shots in golf that you play because there's no other way of finishing close to the hole. The high, cut-up pitch is a good example because it's often the only way to negotiate a hazard, hump, or other form of obstacle – situations where you cannot play a low flying shot.

With a high flight and soft landing, the cut-up pitch is extremely satisfying when you play it well. However, many club golfers fail to succeed with this shot because they think drastic changes in technique are required to produce spectacular results.

This is simply not true. You need to make adjustments to your over-all set-up and swing, but they should be only minor and based on the fundamentals of your normal full swing.

TEMPO IS THE KEY

A smooth swing is essential when you intend lobbing the ball high into the air. The cut-up shot is all about finesse and touch – you must feel in complete control of the clubhead at all times.

To vary the distance you hit the ball with the cut-up pitch, don't vary your tempo in the slightest. As you move closer to the flag, simply shorten your backswing and keep the same rhythm as you would for a longer shot.

Alternatively, grip further down the club – this means you don't have to make any other adjustments to your technique. Shortening the club narrows the arc of your swing which in turn reduces the distance you hit the ball.

If you feel you need to hit the ball hard to generate enough distance, you're probably too far out to play the cut-up pitch shot. It's impossible to maintain control of the ball if all you're thinking about is brute force.

KEEP IN CONTACT

Aim to achieve normal ball to turf contact. You shouldn't feel you need to hit down any more with this shot – your change in set-up and technique should naturally take care of this.

A mistake that many golfers commit is attempting to dig out a huge divot with the sand wedge – mainly because they try to hit down on the ball too hard. The result is a heavy duff. You may see Ian Woosnam knocking doormat divots down the Augusta fairways, but the turf is different from the type you probably play on, and Woosnam is an extremely powerful and talented golfer.

Backswing basics
The full sand wedge is a poorly played shot among many club golfers. Often hit flat out, with the emphasis on taking a divot like a doormat, this shot is miss-hit far more than it should be. The main problem is almost certainly trying to hit the ball out of sight – an effective cure for this fault lies in your backswing.

On the practice green, find out how far you hit your sand wedge, but make only a three-quarter length backswing. Don't swing the club back all the way to horizontal at the top – that's when you start to lose control of the clubhead, and ultimately the ball.

Once you know the distance you hit your sand wedge, and the length of backswing required, you can play the shot with confidence when you're on the course. Never stray too far from this method – you can then develop a more consistent feel for distance from that crucial 100yd (90m) mark.

CUT ABOVE THE REST

1 SELECT YOUR SAND WEDGE
There's a steep rise in front of you, so you need to get the ball up quickly and land it softly on the green the other side. The cut-up chip is perfect, whereas other shots leave too much to chance. To play this master stroke, align slightly open and grip down your sand wedge for control. Make sure the clubface aims straight at the flag.

2 CLUB ON PLANE
Take the club back along a line parallel with your feet. When your hands are about waist high, the shaft of the club should point straight at the flag. Ask a friend to check this point for you – it's an indication that the club is on the correct plane at a crucial stage of the swing.

3 HOW FAR BACK?
Your top of backswing position should vary depending on the length of shot. From around the 50yd (46m) mark you should certainly take the club back beyond halfway – this ensures you can maintain a smooth tempo on the way down.

4 DOWNWARD ATTACK
Your first move from the top determines whether the shot is a success or a failure. You must pull the butt of the club down towards the ball – this sets the necessary angle between your left arm and the shaft of the club to ensure you strike down through impact and don't scoop at the ball.

5 SLIDE RULE
Imagine your left hand leading the clubhead through impact – you want to avoid releasing your hands so that the back of your left faces the target for as long as possible. From greenside rough you're not looking to strike the ball first – the clubhead slides through the grass, inflicting a cushioned blow at impact.

6 CHARGE HAND
Notice how the left hand pulls across the line from out-to-in through impact, not allowing the clubhead to pass the hands at any time. Make sure this is the way you finish every time you play the cut-up shot.

DIFFERENT PERSPECTIVE

VIEW FROM BEHIND

Every golfer knows how difficult it is to judge a shot when you can't see the bottom of the pin. It's a situation that often causes anxiety, which in turn triggers off a bad swing and a poor result.

Viewing the shot from another angle can make all the difference. From behind the pin you can see exactly what you have to do – note factors such as where to land your ball and how much green you have to work

with. Visualize the flight of your ball. Once you have a clear picture in your mind you can then apply the necessary technique best suited to achieving the right result.

Be careful not to hold up play though. In a practice round with no one else present you can take as much time as you like, but when there's a group following close behind, show some consideration and avoid holding them up.

BLIND SHOT OVER HILL
DIFFICULT TO JUDGE

LOOK BACK FROM BEHIND FLAG TO
HELP YOU IDENTIFY LANDING AREA
AND VISUALIZE FLIGHT OF BALL

The Low Sand Wedge

When faced with a pitch shot of 60-80yd (55-73m), it's an advantage to be able to play the ball either high or low. The loft on a sand wedge automatically sends the ball high if the shot is hit properly. But there are times when it's better to play low.

PLAYING A LOW BALL

The low ball is particularly useful when playing into the wind. By moving the ball back in your stance and keeping your hands ahead of the clubhead, you can produce a shot that bores decisively through the wind.

A lower shot is also effective when the ball is lying on a hard, bare surface. This is common on a links course. It's difficult to play a normal high pitch shot when there is no grass under the ball. If the shot isn't played to perfection, the clubhead tends to bounce into

HITTING THE LOW PITCH
Use the low sand wedge for playing into the wind or from a bare lie. You take the loft out of the shot by positioning the ball opposite your right heel at address, and by pushing your hands ahead of the clubhead. Align your body as normal, and grip the club about 1in (2.5cm) from the top. The clubface should be square to the target. For a normal pitch, the ball is central in your stance. In both cases you distribute your weight as normal.

BALL POSITION – LOW PITCH

BALL POSITION – NORMAL PITCH

PLAYING THE LOW PITCH

NORMAL PITCH

① THE TAKEAWAY
For the low sand wedge, your backswing should be a lot shorter than for a normal high shot. There is also very little wrist break. The stroke requires a firm left wrist throughout the shot. Compare this to the backswing for the normal sand wedge, and you'll notice that the club goes past the vertical, and the wrists have broken.

② THE DOWNSWING
Keep your wrists firm and lead the shot with your left arm – unlike the normal pitch where you use your hands conventionally and release into the ball. The main difference between the downswings of the two shots is the relative positions of the club and the hands. Even though your hands are in the same place, the clubhead positions are different.

3 **THE STRIKE**
Notice that the hands are once again in the same place, but the clubhead positions are different. You must keep the clubhead behind your hands during the stroke – unlike the normal shot – and resist the temptation to scoop up the ball. Try to strike the ball fractionally before the ground, nipping it off the turf. This creates the backspin.

4 **THE FOLLOWTHROUGH**
Keep your wrists and arms firm to ensure that your followthrough is short. The feeling of firmness throughout the stroke automatically reduces the loft of your sand wedge, and keeps the ball low. A full followthrough and conventional use of the hands send the ball high. Transfer your weight from the right side to the left during the stroke.

Playing into the wind

Because the natural loft of a sand wedge sends the ball high, it can be difficult to control into a wind. The danger of playing the shot normally is that the ball balloons up in the air and lands short of the target.

The low sand wedge lessens the effect of the wind. The ball pierces the wind, bounces short of the flag and hops up to the hole before biting. The technique for hitting the low wedge naturally creates a lot of backspin, helping you to control the ball.

Even though the ball flies low and looks as if it will go through the back of the green, the effect of the wind and the backspin stops the ball quickly.

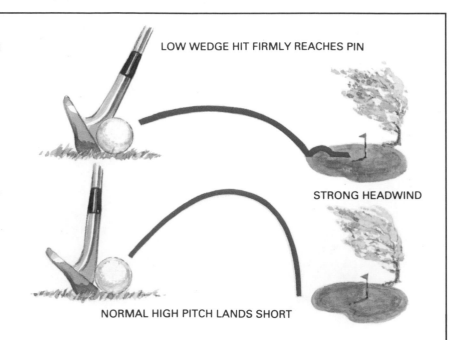

LOW WEDGE HIT FIRMLY REACHES PIN

STRONG HEADWIND

NORMAL HIGH PITCH LANDS SHORT

the ball, resulting in a thinned shot. But the technique you use in hitting the ball low prevents this happening.

CONTROLLED ATTACK

One big advantage is that the shot creates more backspin than normal, giving you greater control. The more control you have, the more aggressive you can be. The shot should be played boldly, and you must never quit on the ball. Failure to attack the ball results in a duffed shot.

When you play the stroke properly, you can be confident of the ball bouncing once and then biting. To onlookers, the shot may seem at first to be a miss-hit. They may feel that the ball is going to fly through the green. It is only when they see the ball checking on the green that they appreciate the shot. This stroke usually causes gasps from the crowd at a big tournament.

Because the shot is played low the ball doesn't stop immediately. You must try to pitch the ball short of the flag, and let it run up to the hole. The distance the ball pitches from the hole varies in different conditions.

If the green slopes towards you or is wet, the ball stops more quickly than normal. Aim to hit the ball further up to the hole. When the green slopes away or is hard, the first bounce should be well short of the flag, allowing the ball to roll up to the hole.

Eamonn Darcy: skilful pitcher
The Irish Ryder Cup player is well known for his prowess near the green. From around 75yd (68m) he is very accurate, and he always gives himself a chance to get up and down in 2.

Darcy naturally hits the ball low, and his slightly stiff style means he is perfectly suited to playing this shot. His flair with the low wedge helped him to second place in the 1989 English Open at The Belfry.

Short and Long Pitch

Approach shots draw gasps of admiration – often tinged with a touch of envy – from the galleries at professional tournaments. Frequently finishing close and sometimes dropping in, the ball seems to have a magical attraction to the hole.

Take heart – any golfer can hit a good approach shot. You don't need bulging forearms, you don't have to possess awesome talent – you just need to have a grasp of the fundamentals. You then have a technique that you can apply to a variety of situations from 100yd (90m) and in.

The short pitch from around 50yd (45m) – often played over some form of hazard – is a shot that frightens many golfers into making a mistake. You need maximum height and minimum roll – there's potentially quite a lot that can go wrong.

Unfortunately it's one of those

CONFIDENCE AND CONTROL
From 100yd (90m) and in, you should find the green every time, get the ball close sometimes and miss the target altogether very rarely. Success from this range hinges a great deal on confidence. However, equally important is control – you must never hit an approach shot flat out. Call on the services of your 9 iron or pitching wedge, grip down the club slightly and make a three-quarter swing.

DOWNHILL APPROACH

WHICH SHOT?
When the fairway slopes downhill to the green and there are no obstacles in the way, you're in the pleasing situation of having a choice of shots. Try to think of a hole on a course you know where the contours are similar, and imagine you're just under 100yd (90m) from the hole. Probably the best shot – and certainly the most consistent – is a low flying, three-quarter stroke with a 9 iron. This controlled shot helps you find the correct line, judge weight accurately, and lets the natural lie of the land sweep your ball down towards the hole.

1 NO FRILLS TECHNIQUE
Golf is such a precise game that you should take every opportunity to keep your technique simple. There are situations when you need to be creative, but there's no call for heroics on this shot. A straightforward address position offers you a technique that is least likely to go wrong – feet, hips and shoulders square to the target with the ball central in your stance.

KEY POINT:
Distribute your weight equally on both feet.

2 EASY BACKSWING
You don't want too many moving parts in your swing here – play a hands and arms shot. Concentrate on a one piece takeaway and keep the club low to the ground. Never pick the club up quickly – you create too steep an arc and are likely to make a poor shoulder turn.

KEY POINT:
Keep it smooth.

(3) CUT DOWN BACKSWING
For a full shot this backswing would be far too short for comfort. In this instance it's the perfect position. Your knees should be comfortably flexed and your shoulders almost fully turned. A little more than half your weight is now on the right side.

KEY POINT:
The left wrist should be firm and in control of the club.

(4) CONSISTENT TEMPO
The most important point to remember at the top of the backswing is that you maintain the same tempo on the way down. Whatever you do don't rush it – this is a major cause of miss-hit shots.

KEY POINT:
Feel the back of your left hand guiding the clubhead.

(5) LEFT SIDE IN CHARGE
Make sure your left wrist is firm through the ball. This ensures that the clubface remains square both into and after impact. A front view provides a good example of how you should retain your height throughout the swing. The head is at exactly the same level now as at address – there's no lifting or dipping at any time.

KEY POINT:
Most of your weight should be on the left foot at impact.

(6) BALANCE PRACTICE
The hard work has already been done, but don't be lazy on the followthrough. Concentrate on key points such as good balance and a comfortable followthrough position. This helps improve your overall tempo during the swing.

KEY POINT:
Your upper body faces the target on the followthrough.

ON THE WATERFRONT

①︎ FLY THE FLAG
With water guarding the front the trouble is all too apparent. The mental fear rather than any degree of difficulty is the downfall of some club golfers. However, from only 60yd (55m), a shot at the flag can make you a contender – if you have the technique you can play a very attacking and satisfying stroke.

KEY POINT:
Grip down the club to enhance control.

②︎ OPEN FOR COMFORT
A slightly open stance is a good idea when you play this shot – your sand wedge is the ideal club. Both combine to produce a higher, more floating trajectory than you would normally wish for. Take the club back along the line of your body and break your wrists earlier than normal – this creates a slightly steeper swing arc which is essential when you play any shot from rough.

KEY POINT:
Keep your right elbow tucked in close to your side.

③︎ SHOULDER TURN
Even on a relatively short shot you need to be certain of making a good shoulder turn – although not quite as full as you would with a driver in your hands. You may be tired of being told to turn your shoulders, but if you don't, you can guarantee the club is way outside the line and on too steep an arc – it's impossible to hit a good shot from there.

KEY POINT:
Point your left knee in towards the ball.

4 UP AND DOWN
A view down the line gives a good indication of how the club should remain on a consistent plane throughout the swing. Note that the hands are in a similar position halfway through the downswing compared to halfway through the backswing. The angle of the club must be different though – almost lagging behind in a position known as a late hit.

KEY POINT:
Keep your head behind the ball – don't lunge forward.

5 STRIKE DOWN
You need lots of height on this shot, so remember to strike down firmly into the bottom of the ball. Compared with the full swing the legs are quite passive. However, they still have a role to play – drive your knees forward through impact to help move your weight on to the left foot. This promotes a sharp downward blow.

KEY POINT:
Keep your hands ahead of the clubhead at all times.

6 DANGEROUS FLOATER
The action of the clubhead sliding through the grass under the ball gives this shot the high, floating trajectory you desperately need. Practice it often – this is a shot that can help you threaten the flag in a host of potentially dangerous situations, such as flying over a hazard.

KEY POINT:
Push the back of your left hand through to the target for as long as possible on the followthrough.

shots that can ruin your score if you play it badly, so you must have the ability to get it right – at least to the extent that your worst pitch finishes very close to the putting surface.

Your sand wedge is the ideal weapon from most lies. Don't make drastic alterations to your technique. Simply open your stance slightly and position the ball further back than normal to ensure a downward blow and crisp contact.

The one exception to this rule is when your ball rests on hardpan. You need a club with a sharper leading edge – such as an 8 or 9 iron – to nip it cleanly off the surface. A sand wedge tends to bounce off hard ground.

PINPOINT ACCURACY

As you move a little further away from the pin, it doesn't necessarily become harder to pitch your ball close.

Professionals probably hit as many shots near to the flag from 100yd (90m) as they do from half that distance. There's no reason why you shouldn't either – although don't expect such a high level of accuracy.

The first point to remember is that it doesn't matter what club you use, as long as the end result is good. This means placing the emphasis on control. There's nothing impressive about bashing a sand wedge to 20ft (6m), if you can knock the ball closer with a comfortable 9 iron.

There are several factors that dictate the type of shot you should play. In calm conditions on a plain, featureless hole you have a wide choice of strokes open to you. In general though, never feel you're using anything more than a three-quarter swing.

FAVORED FLIGHT

It's easy to misjudge a pitch into a green that slopes uphill from front to back. Coming up short is usually the problem for most golfers. Keep backspin out of the shot – it doesn't favor you from this position.

The best policy is to take a less lofted club than usual so that the ball naturally has a bit of run on landing. Pitch it short, but still on the putting surface, and let the ball do the rest. This is your best chance of finishing close to the hole.

Try to avoid playing a high, floating shot in this situation. It demands a very precise stroke to finish close. If you pitch your ball only fractionally short, it's likely to come to an abrupt halt.

If the upslope is severe you may even spin the ball back towards you – particularly if the greens are soft and receptive. This is a disappointing result from a not particularly poor shot.

However, a high trajectory shot is ideal if the green slopes away from you. If you have a good lie you should be able to land the ball softly on the front of the putting surface and allow the slope to carry it gently down towards the hole.

pro tip

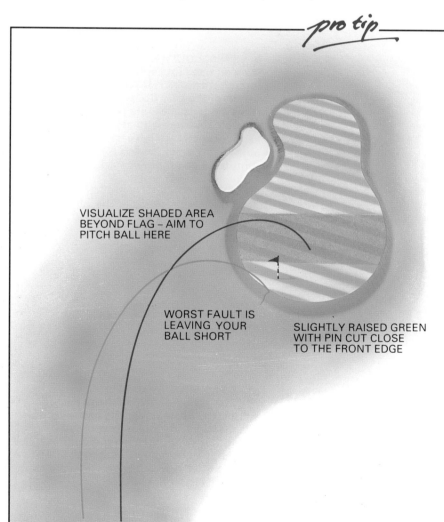

VISUALIZE SHADED AREA BEYOND FLAG – AIM TO PITCH BALL HERE

WORST FAULT IS LEAVING YOUR BALL SHORT

SLIGHTLY RAISED GREEN WITH PIN CUT CLOSE TO THE FRONT EDGE

Percentage pitch
When you're playing well and feeling confident, anywhere under 100yd (90m) can seem like an open invitation to attack the pin. But there are times when it's best to play the percentage pitch.

Raised greens look simple enough and certainly don't inject the same amount of fear as a deep bunker. However, they're cleverly designed, making approach shots deceptively hard. You need to be careful if there are any raised greens on your course.

With the flag positioned close to the front of the green, it's a potentially dangerous situation. Visualize a shaded area just beyond the pin – this is where you should pitch your ball.

Fire too strongly and you finish at the back of the green – play the shot a little too tentatively and you should still find the putting surface. Either way you have a putt rather than a chip for your next shot.

The worst fault is leaving your ball short because you then have to negotiate the slope a second time with your next shot. This is the heavy price you pay for being too impetuous.

Chipping Drills

At the end of the round it's the numbers at the bottom of your card that matter. If you want to score well your short game has to be in good shape. There are no prizes for hitting the ball brilliantly if your total doesn't match your striking ability on the day.

No golfer becomes a good chipper overnight, so take every opportunity to practice this part of your game – your short shots become sharper as a result.

As with all practice, it has to be constructive if you're to reap the full benefits from your efforts. There are probably more practice drills for chipping than any other aspect of golf, so it tends to be more enjoyable. The other advantage is you don't need a great deal of space to chip a few golf balls.

You may also have the boost of holing an occasional chip, which gives you lots of encouragement and spurs you on to hole even more. This form of practice has the psychological edge over hitting full shots – how often do you hole out from 150yd (135m)?

DEVELOPING DRILLS

The purpose of any chipping drill is to discover for yourself which shots work best for you. But there's always a lot to learn from the masters – both in technique and how to visualize each shot.

Tom Watson is a great believer in playing chip shots with as little backspin as possible. He feels that it's easier to roll the ball smoothly and judge pace when there's very little spin on the ball. Only when it's absolutely necessary does Tom aim to stop the ball quickly – for example when there's not much green to work with.

WIDE REPERTOIRE
The best way to learn about shots from close range is to regularly spend time around the practice green. Experiment with different clubs and play a variety of strokes. If you have more than one shot up your sleeve your options are never limited. Whatever the situation, keep your hands ahead of the ball at address and accelerate the clubhead into impact.

MAKE THE CORRECT CHOICE

LEAVE THE FLAG IN...
Every golfer aims to hole greenside chips. While you can't achieve this every time, you can increase the number of shots that finish close by leaving the flag in. This encourages you to be more aggressive on the stroke – you know that even if you hit the ball a little too hard, there's always the possibility of it hitting the flag and occasionally dropping in. This is particularly helpful for downhill chips where the ball often gathers speed towards the hole. Even at pace the ball seldom rebounds too far away, which means your putt is a short one.

...TAKE THE FLAG OUT
If you remove the flag when you chip, you have to judge weight very precisely. In the back of your mind you know the pace has to be spot on for the ball to stand any chance of going in. If you hit the chip too hard there's nothing to stop it – not even the back of the hole – and you're likely to be left with a long putt. You may also find that you leave a lot of chips short. Knowing the ball needs to be rolling gently if it's to drop prompts you to be tentative – which must be the furthest thought from your mind.

There's usually more than one way to play a shot from around the green – club selection is just as important as execution.

For every chip there are two targets you should consider – a precise landing area and the flag. The most accurate way to judge the weight of any chip is first to decide where you want to land the ball and then predict the roll. Don't make the mistake of concentrating *only* on the hole.

Select a hole on the practice green and play shots with a variety of clubs from the same spot. You quickly learn which club is best suited to the shot. You also find out which clubs make it hardest for you to chip the ball close.

An effective way to recreate an on course situation is to play shots to a variety of holes, all from the same spot. There are no second chances in a round of golf, so give yourself only one ball for each chip. This tests your ability to judge line and length at the first attempt. It's also a useful yardstick to assess the development of your touch and feel.

Another productive form of practice is to take a selection of

FLAG LEFT IN – PLAY AN
ATTACKING CHIP AT THE HOLE

BALL STOPPED BY FLAG – MAY DROP IN

CHIP SHOT HIT TOO FIRMLY – BALL
RUNS OVER HOLE

FLAG REMOVED

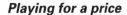

Playing for a price

One of the great advantages of golf is that you can practice on your own. But every now and then you need someone else around to help build a competitive edge into your game.

Chipping provides the perfect opportunity to bet with your friends. Playing for lunch or the first round of drinks is usually just the sort of incentive you need. The stakes aren't high, but no one likes losing.

Select nine different shots to play from around the practice green. The simplest game is playing closest to the hole – keep score as in a matchplay competition. Alternatively, treat each hole as a par 2 and play a mini strokeplay event with just your wedge and a putter.

clubs and a bag of balls and aim to pitch each shot on exactly the same spot. Place a tee peg where you intend landing the ball so you don't lose sight of your objective.

Pay close attention to the differences between each shot – the height generated by each club, the amount of spin on the ball and how far it rolls on landing. This quickly develops your knowledge of chipping and makes it easier to visualize shots when you're on the course.

KEEP IT COMPETITIVE

Even if you're on your own, try to be as competitive as possible in your practice and always set yourself goals. If hitting balls is aimless, you're unlikely to see much of an improvement in your short game – you soon become bored with practicing too.

Treat every chip as a potential matchwinner so that you put pressure on yourself to perform well every time.

Imagine you need to get up and down in two to win the most important competition at your home club. When it comes to the real thing you can look back on the hundreds of times you've been in that situation before – and played a good shot.

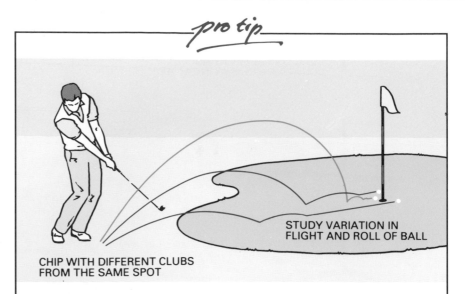

CHIP WITH DIFFERENT CLUBS FROM THE SAME SPOT

STUDY VARIATION IN FLIGHT AND ROLL OF BALL

Choosing the right club

There's more than one way to play a chip shot. When you practice, take a dozen golf balls and play shots to the same hole with a variety of clubs. Only through a process of trial – and an occasional error – do you discover which shots give you the greatest success rate.

The higher the shot the less run there is on landing. This is ideal for floating the ball over trouble and is best played with a sand wedge. However, it's one of the more difficult strokes to play, so avoid the high chip unless you have no option.

Lower shots generate more run on the ball and are perfect when there's no trouble between you and the flag. Ideally, you want the ball running at the hole as smoothly as one of your finest putts. Any club from a 5 iron to an 8 iron gives you enough loft to clear the fringe with very little backspin, promoting roll.

Straight up

When you're just off the edge of the green, check that the flag is standing perfectly vertical in its hole. This makes sure there's a big enough gap for the ball to drop in.

If the flag is leaning slightly towards you it can prevent your ball going in. The rules allow you to straighten the flag so that you're fully rewarded if you play a good shot. But don't be greedy – you're not allowed to deliberately lean the flag away from you.

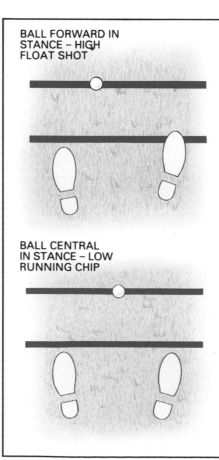

BALL FORWARD IN STANCE – HIGH FLOAT SHOT

BALL CENTRAL IN STANCE – LOW RUNNING CHIP

Altering ball position

Your stance and ball position have just as much bearing on a chip as the club you use. Subtle alterations to both enable you to vary your shots without changing your club.

If you want to float the ball high and stop it quickly, open your stance and position the ball just opposite your inside left heel. You can use your normal bunker shot technique to slide the clubhead under the ball, slightly out-to-in.

Playing the ball further back in your stance lets you use the same club to hit a lower shot. This is particularly helpful if the ball is sitting down in light rough.

Make sure the clubface is square to the target – this delofts the club and contributes to the lower trajectory of the shot. Break your wrists early on the backswing and strike down firmly with your hands leading into impact.

Avoid Green Tension

Of all the strokes in golf, holing a putt just when you really need to gives you the greatest psychological lift. You know you can do it, but pressure has a nasty habit of undermining every golfer's technique at some time or other – no matter how good or confident the player happens to be.

If you can stay relaxed on the greens in a competition, your putting stroke remains with you all the way to the 18th hole of the match. Avoiding green tension is the key to putting well under pressure.

Cast your mind back to a couple of your best competition rounds – your putting was probably on song. On days like this – when the hole looks like a bucket – the putts

HOLING OUT UNDER PRESSURE

There are many ways to avoid tension on the greens – it's essential you have a system that works for you. If you can stay relaxed on the greens your putting is more likely to stand up to the most intense pressure. Whether it's a shortish putt on the 18th to secure a good score, or a curling left to righter to win a match, you can be confident of knocking it in.

STRAIGHT AND NARROW

WELL STRUCK PUTT
ROLLS BALL
STRAIGHT AT HOLE

RAISED RIDGES VARY IN WIDTH
AROUND EACH BALL

The perfect putting stroke strikes the ball slightly upwards with the putter face square to the intended line – the result is a smooth roll on the ball.

A set of three golf balls is manufactured, each with a raised ridge around its circumference. The idea is to set each ball rolling perfectly straight without it toppling over to one side – achieve this and you know a putt is correctly hit.

Start practicing with the ball that has the widest ridge – this is the easiest of the three and gives you some early confidence. As you become more proficient move on to the next ball with a narrower ridge. If you perform this exercise successfully with the final ball, you can be confident that your putting stroke is in pretty good shape.

If you can't find these golf balls at a pro shop near you, paint a stripe around one of your practice balls. Take a putt with the stripe aiming straight at the hole. If it continues to point along the same line for its entire journey, you've struck the ball squarely and correctly.

Any sidespin – the ruin of every missed putt – is unmistakable as the stripe becomes more of a blur than a straight line.

SMOOTH STROKE

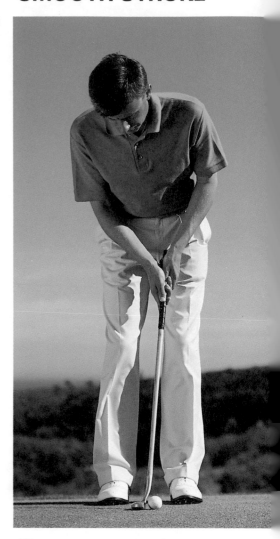

(1) RELAXED OVER THE BALL
Staying relaxed at address is one of the keys to success over a long putt. Position the ball opposite your left heel – this helps you to stroke the ball slightly on the up to give it overspin. Your hands should be at least level with the ball – ahead is fine but behind is potentially disastrous.

pro tip

Shake to relax
Making sure your muscles are free from tension is essential when you're on the green. Relaxation promotes feel and touch – two vital qualities to good putting. If you struggle to achieve this, a simple exercise might solve the problem.

Before you address the ball, rest your putter against your leg and allow your arms to hang down freely. Loosely shake your hands a couple of times to relieve any muscle tightness – when it comes to standing over the ball you should be nicely relaxed.

② SMOOTHLY BACK
Maintaining a light grip, sweep the putter back low away from the ball. Make sure the triangle formed by your shoulders and arms remains the same as at address. For a putt of this length try to keep your wrists firm. If you allow them to hinge it's easy to lose control of the putter head – this upsets the angle of the clubface at a critical moment during the stroke.

③ DOWN AND THROUGH
Accelerate the putter smoothly into impact – the ball position at address ensures the clubhead travels up and generates overspin to set the ball rolling. If you hit down on a putt the ball usually hops into the air, making it extremely difficult to judge pace. Keep your left wrist firm to ensure your hands are in front of the putter head for as long as possible.

tend to drop at crucial stages in the round. This is the difference between a potentially winning score and an average one.

Because you have to be more precise on the greens than elsewhere on the course, tension is disastrous. It destroys the most important ingredient of any putting stroke – feel.

Your putter starts to behave erratically as you struggle to control the line and length of even the simplest of putts. You're in for a frustrating time as the ball keeps slipping past the hole.

TENSION TRIGGERS

There are several causes of ten-sion on the greens. On a **good round** in a competition there are many pressures on you to keep your score intact. Probably the greatest of these is remaining solid when it comes to the business of holing out.

When your **confidence is low** it's easy to imagine the hole is almost shrinking before your eyes – knocking in a putt of any real distance can seem like the hardest task in the world.

This doubt often stems from missing a short putt or two early in the round – your confidence has taken a battering.

The golfing muscles can also tighten at the prospect of a **difficult putt**. Every golfer has a ten-sion trigger – the one that breaks from left to right is the most commonly disliked.

Perhaps you find that putts from one particular range are the stuff that nightmares are made of. And a downhill putt on a slippery green is a real test of nerve, even for the professionals.

Whatever green experience triggers tension for you, don't be reconciled to disaster. Rather than expecting the worst, set out to break your run of missed putts.

Even if you've never felt the slightest bit nervous over a putt – which is unlikely – certain techniques promote a reliable putting stroke when it really matters. Striking your putt within a well rehearsed groove makes all the difference.

The hands play a vital role in the putting stroke, so first examine your grip. Do you feel in control of the clubhead? There's no right or wrong way to hold a putter – styles depend on individual taste and preference.

Making a good stroke

In the winter months greens are naturally more bumpy than in hot, sunny conditions. The grass tends to be a bit woolly which prevents the ball from rolling smoothly. You're bound to see the occasional good putt wander off line on an uneven surface.

In these conditions concentrate on making a good stroke at the ball and don't worry too much if the putts don't drop. It's easy to start doubting your putting stroke – thinking there's something wrong with you when often it's the greens that are at fault. Try to be patient and avoid changing your technique or your putter – good greens are usually just round the corner.

If you're a wristy putter – rather in the style of Gary Player – always grip the club lightly in both hands. The same applies if – like Tom Watson for instance – you're a shoulders and arms putter. Never grip the club too tightly – it restricts your feel for the clubhead, making assessment of weight tricky.

GRIP PRESSURE

Check your grip pressure is the same throughout the stroke. A consistently light grip helps you to make a smooth stroke and accurately judge the weight of a putt – it also reduces the risk of the putter face opening or closing.

To achieve success on the greens you need a sound putting stroke. Though you can copy certain fundamentals from the professionals, there should always be a personal touch to your putting if you're to be comfortable.

Only if a style is your own can you feel truly comfortable over the ball. A natural stance is a real tension beater – if there's a key to holing more putts, this is it. Sticking rigidly to one particular technique can hold back your putting.

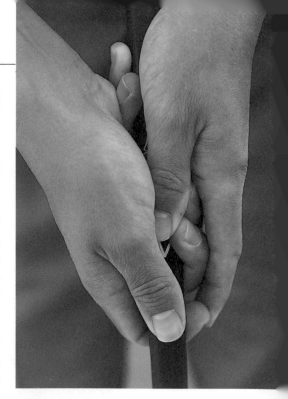

PALMS FACING
You have the perfect putting grip when both hands work in harmony throughout the stroke. The reverse overlap – the most commonly used putting grip – is one of the best ways to achieve this. Both thumbs point straight down the shaft with the palms facing each other. A constant grip pressure encourages the hands to operate as one unit.

pro tip

Stroke of genius

Major championships are the ultimate test of nerve for professionals – some cope and others crumble. Few golfers experience such pressures, but you can learn a valuable lesson just by watching.

When Seve Ballesteros strode on to the final green in the 1984 Open at St. Andrews, he knew if he holed the 12ft (4m) putt the title was his.

Because Seve's putting style is his own he is able to feel comfortable over the ball. Even under intense pressure his stance is relaxed and his grip free from tension. A smooth, unhurried stroke saw the ball drop in the right edge of the hole – the claret jug was his for the second time.

When you're faced with an important putt, take time to compose yourself. Make a couple of practice strokes to give you a feel for the distance and, most important, to relax your muscles. Few experiences in golf are more satisfying than holing a putt when it matters.

Try Out Putting Grips

All golfers go through periods of losing their putting touch and confidence on the greens. They may not twitch or yip the putts but just don't seem to hole as many as they should.

By experimenting with your putting grip you may find one that helps recapture your lost touch, and leads you to hole more putts. It's probably only a case of fine tuning.

CONSISTENT STROKES

The aim is to find a putting grip that is comfortable and helps you repeat your stroke consistently. This repetition of a smooth stroke is the most important part of a good putting game.

Remember that the hands play a passive role in the putting stroke. They must grip the club lightly yet hold the putter steady at all times – the hands shouldn't take any part in swinging the club. Adopt a grip that restricts any wrist action – a cause of much poor putting. Let the arms and shoulders swing the

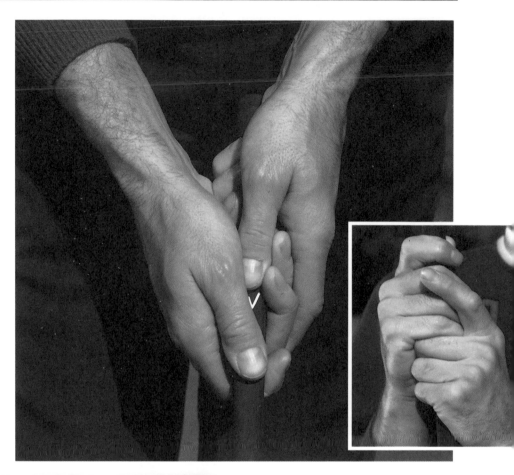

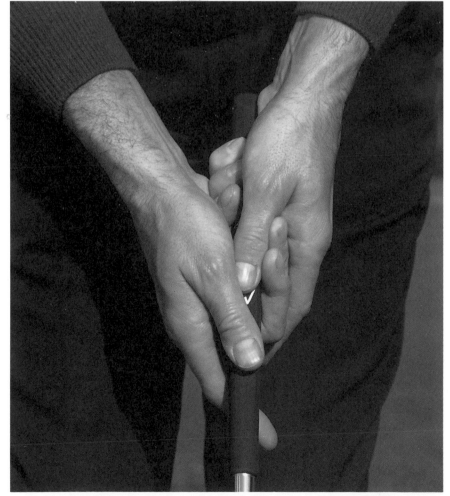

▲ STANDARD REVERSE OVERLAP
Try placing the forefinger of your left hand over either your little finger or all the fingers of your right hand. This restricts the breaking of the left wrist. Point your thumbs down the grip so your palms are square to the target. Players such as Crenshaw, Watson, Lyle and Nicklaus use grips very similar to this.

◄ OVERLAP CONTROL
Both Ballesteros and Faldo also favor the reverse overlap grip, with one variation. The forefinger of the right hand points down the grip and curls slightly underneath. This makes the right hand a little more passive, curbing the tendency to pull putts. Seve feels that this also gives him better feel and control on longer putts.

UNORTHODOX GRIPS

SPLIT HANDED

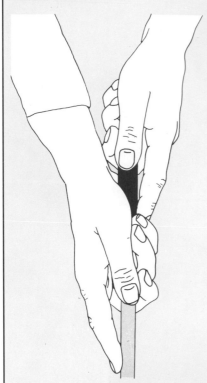

You may find an unorthodox grip works best. Try **splitting your hands** on the shaft – like Hubert Green – so that the right hand guides the stroke. Or try the cross-handed and the baseball grip. The **cross-handed** grip ensures that the left hand steers the shot and adds the power. The **baseball grip** is where all ten fingers are placed on the putter, giving the left and right hands equal prominence.

CROSS HANDED

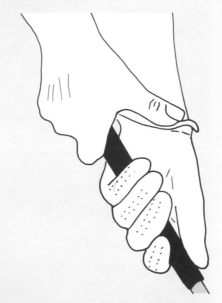

BASEBALL

putter throughout the stroke.

Concentrate on holing out from around 10ft (3m) when you experiment with different grips. This is the crucial distance you must master to lower your scores. Try to find the grip that helps you to hole this length of putt more often – a good smooth stroke from this range should carry on to your longer putts as well.

Most of the world's top players have experimented with their putting grip at some time. The secret to their success is that they have found one they feel confident with, and can consistently reproduce a good stroke. But some players who have a history of troubles on the greens still constantly change their style, hoping their putting improves.

There are no hard and fast rules about which grip you should play with – it's what works best for you. But there are a few basic styles, which most amateurs and professionals use. These are well worth experimenting with until you find one you like.

Langer's yip tip
The long hitting German has had his problems on the greens over the years – he has constantly experimented with different putting grips. A recent style is one Langer himself devised. He grips down the club with his left hand and then clasps the grip and his left forearm together with his right hand.

Langer turned to this unusual style to cure the yips. The left arm is locked on to the club making it impossible for the left wrist to break. He has had some success since turning to these drastic measures – he won the 1990 Madrid Open.

Crenshaw: Master Putter

T he gentle Texan Ben Crenshaw is acknowledged by his fellow professionals and golfing experts as the best putter in the world. He studied the technique of Bobby Jones to help develop his near perfect stroke. Crenshaw's touch is legendary – he putts well on even the most difficult greens.

Believing putting to be an art not a science, Ben relies on simple fundamentals – he never allows himself to get bogged down in the more remote complexities of technique. The result is a pure and natural stroke.

PUTT PRIORITIES

The 1984 Masters champion recommends a putting style that suits the individual but is based on correct principles – a comfortable grip that keeps the blade square, a smooth arm swing and good feel.

You need to combine sound basic technique with an ability to read the greens. Ben accepts that speed determines the line when gauging a putt, and poorly judged speed rather than line is the cause of most three putts.

TEXAN TALENT
Ben Crenshaw combines a natural talent for judging slope and pace with superb technique, and is one of the game's finest putters. Both his long approach putts and touch around the hole are masterly.

Controlled comfort
Crenshaw holds the putter with a light and perfectly balanced grip. Both thumbs point down the shaft, leaving his hands square to the target line. His wrists stay firm throughout the stroke.

He believes every golfer should find a comfortable grip – one that works for the individual, rather than following a style that suits someone else. But try out the Texan's method, adapting it to your own game, if you're struggling to hole putts.

BOTH THUMBS DOWN SHAFT

Trust your first instincts when reading greens is Crenshaw's advice. On long putts, worry about the weight of the shot more than the line – a putt that's the right distance is never far away. He treats short putts as 70% line and 30% feel. Keeping his head down until he hears the putt drop, he thinks about the stroke rather than the hole.

SMOOTH TEMPO

You can learn a lot from watching Crenshaw. He uses an arm rather than a wristy stroke. This makes his striking consistent – you must have perfect timing to putt well with a wrist stroke. Ben's action is smooth and the tempo is constant throughout the swing.

The Texan's grip is conventional – a reverse overlap. He points his thumbs down the shaft, ensuring that his hands are square to the target, and keeps the putter blade square throughout the stroke.

Like many top pros, he positions the ball opposite his left heel to promote a good roll. Although Crenshaw plays with a perfect pendulum stroke, his stance is slightly less standard.

Most top golfers position the ball so that their eyes are directly over it. But Ben putts with the ball further away from his body. He feels that this gives him the free-dom to swing his arms rhythmi-cally with no restrictions.

PUTTING LANE

When Ben visualizes a putt he doesn't just imagine a line, he sees a lane the width of the hole. This makes him feel more confident – he knows if he sets the ball off down the lane with the proper speed it has a chance of going in.

If you're struggling with your putting, go back to the basics. Even Crenshaw loses his sur-geon's precision now and again, but he persists with the simple techniques he's always used. Don't despair if your putts aren't dropping – if they keep coming close they'll eventually go in.

Ben hasn't become the putter he is by just playing – he's worked for hours on the practice putting green to perfect his stroke. Follow his example – work out a practice routine involving both easy and difficult long and short putts.

PROVEN PUTTING STYLE

Use the basics but don't be afraid to experiment is Crenshaw's advice. The Ryder Cup player adopts a near standard technique on the greens. The only part of his set-up that is slightly unconventional is his ball position. Although he places the ball opposite his left heel – as many top golfers do to promote good roll – he plays it well away from his body.

Most golf teachers say that your eyes should be directly over the ball at address so that you can see the line easily. But Ben's method is effective, giving his arms the freedom to swing in a relaxed way. Crenshaw provides evidence that sound basics and an individual style are a powerful combination.

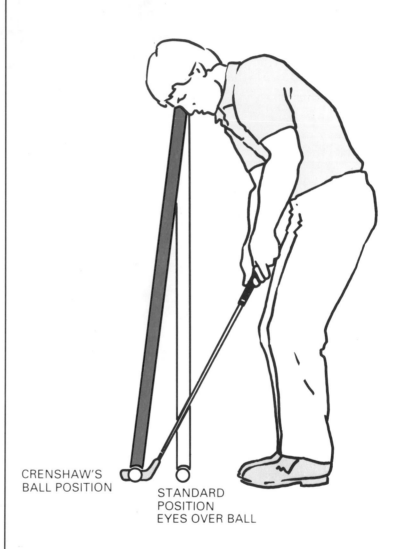

CRENSHAW'S BALL POSITION

STANDARD POSITION EYES OVER BALL

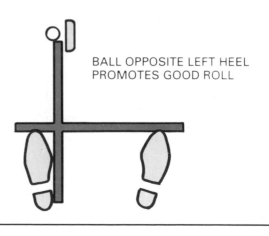

BALL OPPOSITE LEFT HEEL PROMOTES GOOD ROLL

Sloping Putts

Approaching a sloping putt well briefed and in the right frame of mind is the best way to hole it.

Many simple-looking holes are strengthened by heavily contoured greens, so make life easier for yourself by taking precautions.

ASSESS THE GREEN

Many parkland courses have relatively flat greens – you can deal with these fairly easily if you have a smooth putting stroke.

Heathland and links courses are a more complicated matter – their greens are designed to make you concentrate until your ball disappears into the hole.

When top players practice before a tournament, they size up the green from all angles. Putting from every part of the green helps them learn the best spot on which to land their approach shots – if they're on target they can look forward to a birdie putt.

You can make putting on sloping greens a lot easier by copying the pros. If you play the same course regularly, make a note of the best and worst parts of the greens. Aim your approach shots to the areas which offer the straightest putts.

Don't be content to hit the green anywhere – the most inviting spot may leave a three-putt.

GREEN SPEED

To assess how much the ball will move on a slope, you must get a feeling for the speed of the green. If the speed of the practice green

USE THE PIN
Play a sloping putt smoothly and confidently. Have the flag attended if it helps you gauge the slopes – though the pin must be removed after you've hit the ball.

Shade your eyes
To concentrate on the line of your putt, crouch down on your haunches and shade your eyes as you read the green. This helps give you a clearer, better defined picture of the putt you have to make than a wide and distracting view of the whole green – which disturbs your concentration.

PUTTING ACROSS A SIDESLOPE

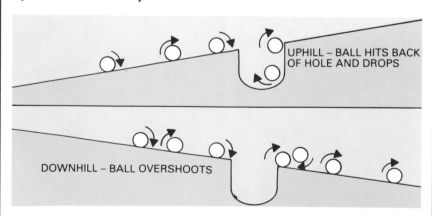

READ THE PUTT
After you've read your putt play a smooth, straight shot along your imaginary ball-to-target line.

SPEED AND LINE
Some sloping putts have a huge borrow. Both speed and line have to be spot on if you're to get the ball close.

LET IT ROLL DOWN
Your ball-to-target line should account for the slope, so that a straight putt along your chosen path rolls down to the hole of its own accord.

is the same as the greens on the course where you play, spend some time putting beforehand. You'll putt far more confidently during your round.

The speed of your putt affects its line. A softly struck putt reacts to the subtle slopes more acutely than a firmly hit shot. If the green is fast, hit softly so that you don't overhit – allow for movement.

Bear in mind that a putt will not swing as far on a wet green as it does on dry grass. A putt on a wet green may leave a track in the grass as well, which gives an excellent indication of the swing.

Look at your putt from all angles to check the line – one view on its own could deceive.

Whatever the slope on your line, hit your putts straight. Let the borrow you've allowed roll your ball towards the hole. Never try to curve or spin a putt. Keep a positive image of the line in your mind and hit smoothly.

Uphill and downhill putts

UPHILL – BALL HITS BACK OF HOLE AND DROPS

DOWNHILL – BALL OVERSHOOTS

Always try to give yourself an uphill putt rather than a downhill one. A fast uphill putt that hits the back of the hole may still drop in. But a speedy downhill putt is risky – even if it's dead on line the momentum may send your ball flying over the hole and off into the distance.

Putting on Two Tiers

When your approach shot lands on one tier and the flag is on the other, you should still need no more than two putts. Learning to putt well on a two-tier green saves precious strokes.

Although the putting technique is the same as on a flat green, judging the bank is the key to playing well. Understanding how a ball behaves when it rolls over the step is half the battle.

Going straight up or down the bank is purely a matter of judging how hard to hit the ball. But when you're faced with a putt across the green and over the bank the line must be taken into account.

CHANGING PATHS

The path of the ball changes twice on its way to the hole. It first alters when the ball runs on to the bank between the tiers, and changes again when the putt reaches the other tier. The final path is parallel to the initial line.

For example, if you need to putt

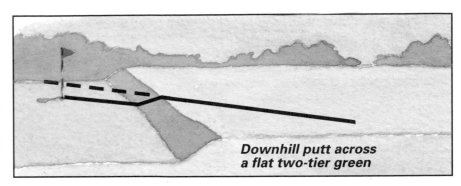

Downhill putt across a flat two-tier green

Uphill putt across a sloping two-tier green

TWO PUTT ZONE

WEAK PUTT

AVOID THREE PUTTING
Putting on split level greens needs careful thought to calculate the pace and line of the ball.

For a **downhill putt** going across a flat two-tier green from left to right you must aim to the right of the hole. The bank turns the ball left but it straightens out towards the hole on reaching the lower tier. The path the ball takes on the lower tier is parallel to the initial line if you judge the pace correctly.

When going **up the bank** aim to hit the ball into an imaginary two putt zone around the hole. Remember to take into account the cross slope on the top tier.

You must always get the ball on to the top tier with your first putt, even if it goes past the hole. Never hit the ball too weakly so it rolls back down the slope – a three putt is almost a certainty.

up and across – from left to right – a two-tier green, you must aim at a point wide and left of the hole. The ball moves to the right on the bank then straightens again when it reaches the top tier.

The amount the ball breaks depends on how high and steep the bank is, and the pace of the putt. The higher the bank, the more the ball moves off line, and the wider of the hole you must aim. The ball is less affected by the bank if it's rolling fast. If the green also slopes across, take this into account when choosing your line.

Once you have chosen your line you must judge the pace.

If you're **going downhill** pick a point on the edge of the bank and try to hit your ball over it. Imagine you're putting to a hole on the step. The strength of the putt should be just enough for the ball to trickle over.

Make sure the ball reaches the lower tier every time – a ball 10ft (3m) past the hole is better than leaving it on the top tier. If the hole is a long way from the foot of the bank, aim at a point on the bottom tier to make certain the ball reaches the target.

When **putting uphill** onto the top tier, choose a spot past the hole to counter the effect of the bank. Imagine you're playing to a hole beyond the actual flag. If you judge the pace correctly and take the proper line the ball should finish fairly close to the pin. You can lag your first putt to give an easy second.

Judgement putting

When faced with a putt on a two-tier green you must make sure that you two putt – with practice it isn't that difficult. Fix your mind on avoiding the three putt – regard holing your first putt as a bonus.

To calculate the pace and line coming across the green and down a bank you must understand how the step and any slope affect the ball. Aim slightly right of the flag – visualize putting to an imaginary target at the top of the bank. The ball is carried away naturally by the bank towards the hole.

DOWN AND ACROSS
TWO-TIER GREEN

IMAGINARY TARGET

Canny Canizares

In the 1989 Ryder Cup match, José-Maria Canizares had two putts from 55ft (17m) on the 18th to retain the trophy for Europe. But he had to come downhill over a bank – judgement was all important.

He stroked the putt perfectly so it just rolled to the edge of the bank and then trickled down to within 3ft (1m) of the hole. He holed the next to beat Ken Green and secure the tie.

Judging the Grain

Although reading the green correctly is essential, you can hole even more putts by judging the grain properly.

The grain is the direction in which the grass grows. In mild climates, grass grows straight up, so the grain hardly affects your putt. However, the grass is mown up and down, pushing it in one direction and then the other. These stripes give the same effect as natural grain.

EFFECTS OF GRAIN
The same putt varies according to the grain (the direction in which the grass grows or is mown). In warm climates, the natural grain can slow down, speed up or curve a putt. Mowing the grass can have a similar effect in colder climates.

WITH THE GRAIN
If the grass is pale, you are putting with the grain, and your ball travels quickly.

AGAINST THE GRAIN
The same putt hit against the grain runs more slowly and falls short of the hole.

ACROSS THE GRAIN
As the putt meets the join it is almost like hitting a wall. The ball veers as a result.

ACROSS THE GRAIN
The putt curves away as it strikes the join, along the left-to-right line of the mini "wall."

A green with a strong grain looks dull and dark when you stand on one side, and shiny and light from the other. When it looks light and shiny, you are putting with the grain, and the ball runs very quickly. With the green looking dull and dark, a putt is against the grain and runs relatively slowly.

In warmer countries, such as Australia, South Africa and the holiday areas of southern Europe, the natural grain is pronounced. Recognizing it and understanding what it does to the ball's path is as important as gauging the slope and line of your putt.

READING THE GRAIN

Golf courses in hot countries usually have greens laid with either Bermuda or bent grass. These are grasses which shoot up quickly in the sun and also grow in specific directions.

The direction the grass grows depends on where the green is – if there is sea or a natural lake nearby, it's very likely that the grain leads towards it.

Alternatively, the grain may point where the prevailing wind is heading, or it could lead away from mountains. Taking all these factors into account is vital if you are putting on grainy greens.

SLOPE AND GRAIN

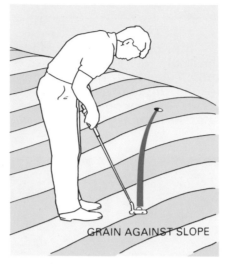

GRAIN AGAINST SLOPE

GRAIN WITH SLOPE

When the green slopes downwards and the grain runs against the slope, the putt is almost straight. If both the slope and the grain run in the same direction, the line of your putt becomes more acute. You must allow for even more break and aim well to the left of the hole.

The same goes for the stripes left by a mower. You need to assess the grass direction before you can judge the pace of your putt correctly. The ball has to roll over the join between each stripe, so you also have to allow for this making your putt break.

An uphill putt against the grain is extra slow. But the same putt with the grain may counteract the effect of the slope, and make a normal – or fast – stroke.

If the grain runs sideways across the line of your putt, it has the same effect as a sideslope. This means curving the putt with the grain.

If you have a left-to-right putt, and the grain runs in the same direction, the break becomes even more acute. When the line of your putt goes against the grain, its break is almost cancelled.

Ben Crenshaw: master putter
Ben Crenshaw is widely regarded as the most successful putter in modern golf. He is living proof of the old golf saying, "Drive for show, putt for dough."

On occasions, when Crenshaw's erratic swing isn't working too reliably, he stays in contention in many tournaments because of his beautifully tuned putting stroke.

Crenshaw putts so well because he perfected the firm-wristed pendulum action. He is also a superb green reader. Knowing that the slightest misjudgment can make a putt lip out, he studies the green and the grain from all angles until he is sure of his pace and line.

The confidence that comes from assessing the grain and slopes accurately is essential to playing a positive stroke.

Dry or damp?
A hot sun dries out the grass very quickly. If the green is sunken, or has trees overhanging it, parts of it may remain in shadow for longer than others. This means that sections of the same green can be either bone dry or damp.

Remember this when you assess your putt – damp grass can slow the ball down considerably, while dryness means a fast putt and a more acute break.

Green Drills

Putting practice is vital, but still there isn't as much time spent on it as there should be. What can put people off is the boredom of hitting stroke after stroke at a hole.

You need to make putting practice enjoyable while improving your touch naturally. Using various drills and games helps you to become a better judge of line and weight, and to groove your stroke without unnecessary toil and boredom.

Many useful drills don't involve a hole at all, and some need more than one person to be of any use. Try to find the ones that you enjoy most, but also those that work on the worst aspects of your putting game – perhaps judgment of distance.

It's important to develop all facets of your putting game so you're solid from both short and long range – not just in a friendly game but when the heat is on and the pressure of competition is fierce.

MEASURED WEIGHT
To find your feel for distance it's best not to aim at a hole – it can be distracting. To gauge long range putts, simply press a tee peg into the practice green and try to lay every putt dead – within 2ft (60cm). Playing with a couple of friends helps as well – score a point every time you knock your ball closest to the tee. Perhaps even play for a small wager to help you cope with pressure.

To develop a touch for medium range putts, lay out three tee pegs in a line, the first about 15ft (4.5m) away and then at 10ft (3m) intervals. Hit two balls at each peg and keep repeating the exercise. This teaches you to take a putt on individually and judge the pace each time, which helps your touch.

▶ **BOWLING GREEN**
One of the most enjoyable ways to hone your judgment of pace and line is to play bowls. You need two or more players, three balls each and a jack – the target ball. Player 1 knocks the jack down the green, then hits his first ball towards it, trying to go as close as possible. Player 2 then has to beat his rival. Take alternate shots until you have hit all the balls.

To score, judge whose ball is closest. If you have the nearest ball award yourself a point. If two balls are closer than your rival's nearest, award two points. And if you are lucky enough to have knocked three inside your opponent's, claim three points. Play until one of you has reached 21.

Allen's drill
US pro Michael Allen uses a very simple but effective practice aid to groove his putting stroke. He lays two clubs down parallel to each other – at just over putter head width apart – and aligns them at the hole, so that if he hits a straight putt the ball drops.

This means he has to take the putter back on a straight line or else it collides with the clubs on the ground. But he must also keep the blade square to target back and through the ball if the putt is to drop.

Allen's hard work on his putting finally paid dividends in 1989 when he won the Scottish Open. Five strokes back with one round to play he shot an amazing 63 to pip Ian Woosnam and José-Maria Olazabal. With 7 birdies and an eagle in the last 13 holes he needed only 22 putts.

He ended the year tied for 9th in the putting statistics – averaging under 30 putts per round – and carried this form to the US Qualifying School where he earned his card for 1990.

▼ **ALL IN A ROW**
Although trying to hole out every time isn't always a good idea – because you can easily become bored and lose your confidence – one drill works well on the short putts. Line five or six balls up on a flat piece of green about 12in (30cm) apart, starting from 3ft (1m) out.

Attempt to hole the first ball. If you do, move on to the next, and so on until you fail to hole out. When you fail, retrieve all the balls and start again. The object of the exercise is to hole out every ball one after the other. This drill helps your short putt stroke and does wonders for your concentration and determination. It makes you really want to hole out each time as you know you must start all over again if one fails to drop.

pro tip

Sweeten your touch

WEIGHTING GAME

To ensure accurately weighted putts, it's critical to cultivate your touch and feel from medium and long range. Your muscles rely on being sent a precise message from your brain about how hard to hit the putt.

To help you ingrain a sense of distance and weight into your game, forget about the line of your putts for a moment. Go on to the practice green with about ten balls and position yourself 15ft to 40ft (4.5-12m) away from the edge. Then putt each ball towards the fringe – playing to a hole distracts your gauging of weight as you have to think about the line of the putt as well. Try to stop the ball as close as possible to the edge of the green without ever running up on to the fringe.

Play against someone else to make it more interesting – perhaps for a little wager – and score a point every time you knock one closest to the edge.

The action of putting to a band rather than a hole naturally helps your perception and feel for length. This drill should give you confidence to judge long range putts out on the course and avoid the dreaded 3 putt.

BLIND MAN'S PUTT
Putting without ever looking up to see where the ball has gone is a remarkably tell-tale drill. It gives you an accurate indication of your natural feel for weight.

With roughly ten balls, aim to a hole-free area. Take one ball at a time and try to stroke it to a point about 25ft (7.5m) away. Don't look up between shots, just roll the next ball towards you and repeat your stroke. Try to keep everything the same – the line, rhythm and strength. The idea is to finish up with the balls as tightly grouped as possible.

Only after the last ball is on its way may you look up. With putts of that length you should be able to throw an imaginary ring – about 2 ft (75cm) in diameter – around all the balls. Keep practicing until you succeed, then move on to a longer distance. For every 5ft (1.5m) you add to the length of the putt, the diameter of your target area should increase by 6in (15cm).

This drill is better than the usual blindfold exercise – putting with your eyes shut – since you can still concentrate on your stroke, and your ball striking is more consistent. Both your touch and putting stroke improve together.

Bunker Positioning

Every golfer has suffered a traumatic experience in sand before – either by being too delicate, or attempting too much and coming to grief. Whatever the cause, it always comes as a major disappointment. Avoid experiences like this by reducing the number of visits you make to sand.

The key lies more in your mind than in your golf bag. You need a cool, calculated approach – a strategy that prevents you doing just what the course designer wanted you to do.

SIDESTEP THE SAND

Fairway bunkers are designed to make you think off the tee. Instead of looking at them as a potential problem, use these bunkers to your advantage. Fairway bunkers can help you visualize a specific

CAVALIER APPROACH

If you're unfortunate enough to land in a bunker, don't lose heart – sand is a better proposition than water or out of bounds. When it's a fairway bunker you can afford to be adventurous – they're often shallow which means you can take a long club. Firing from long range, think of the club you would take from the same distance off grass and choose one more. Then enjoy the moment as your ball sails towards the green.

NOTHING TO GAIN

▶ **Many short par 4s are cunningly designed to catch you out. The holes look innocent enough, but the lack of length is often more than made up for by cleverly placed bunkers. Play the percentages to make sure you don't fall into the course designer's trap.**

Off the tee, select a club that guarantees your ball pulls up short of the fairway bunkers – even if you hit your Sunday best drive. This means the sand poses no threat. A good shot leaves you a straightforward approach into the green and sets you up for an excellent birdie opportunity.

If you risk all off the tee, you've very little to gain and everything to lose. Even with your best drive you still need an element of luck to avoid the sand and the chances of finding the green are slim. If it's not your day the ball may plummet into the sand, leaving you a medium range bunker shot – one of the hardest strokes in golf. What looks like a birdie opportunity on the card suddenly turns into a careless dropped shot.

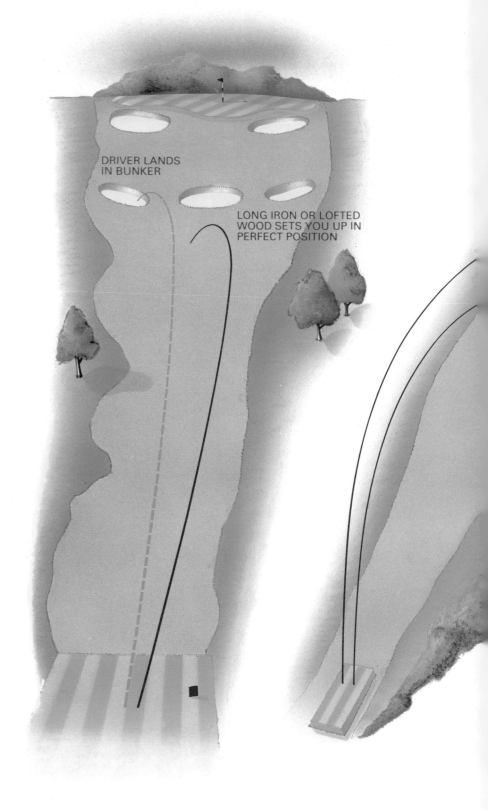

DRIVER LANDS IN BUNKER

LONG IRON OR LOFTED WOOD SETS YOU UP IN PERFECT POSITION

shot.

Also bear in mind that on most courses fairway traps are usually quite shallow and easy to escape from. The exceptions to this rule tend to be links courses where deep pot bunkers pose a serious threat to your score.

If you're sensible about club selection you should always be able to avoid cross bunkers. Positioned at the distance most golfers hit their drivers, there's usually no going around them – the only choice you have to make is whether to lay up short or try and carry them.

Whatever your decision, always give yourself a bit of leeway. If a 3 wood lands you perilously close to the sand, choose a more lofted club just to be safe. Only decide to carry cross bunkers if you can achieve it without forcing the shot.

An isolated fairway bunker you know you can comfortably carry is an ideal marker to help you line

up. Find a spot on the tee that lets you fire straight over the bunker to achieve perfect position on the fairway beyond.

Bunkers in the distance can also play a useful part in the lining up process. If they're out of reach, set your sights on the sand and fire away. Aiming at a specific mark in

the distance is a good habit to build into your game.

Often when there's a clear fairway ahead, it's easy to blast away merrily thinking it's impossible to find trouble. This is the sort of careless approach that leads to your sloppiest drive – disaster is usually lurking just round the corner.

IN THE DRIVING SEAT

ONLY ADVENTUROUS DRIVE CLEARS SAND TO OPEN UP GREEN FOR SECOND SHOT

SAFE TEE SHOT PULLS UP SHORT OF THE BUNKERS

◀ The temptation on a long par 4 is always to drive the ball out of sight – after all, the closer you are to the green the easier your second shot. But this is only true if you're on the fairway – there's no advantage gained if your ball ends up in sand.

When fairway bunkers guard the landing area on a par 4, it's wise to lay up short of them with a lofted wood. Even though you leave yourself a longer shot into the green, at least you can play off grass. If you're 20yd (18m) nearer the green but in the bunker, the shot is a lot harder. It may even be impossible to reach in two.

If you're feeling adventurous reach for your driver and fire past the bunkers. The reward is great – a shorter shot at the flag. But the price of failure is a high one – little or no chance of reaching the green in regulation.

HAZARDOUS PAR 3

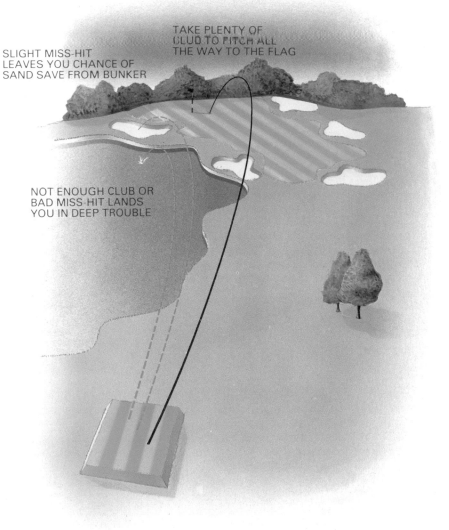

TAKE PLENTY OF CLUB TO PITCH ALL THE WAY TO THE FLAG

SLIGHT MISS-HIT LEAVES YOU CHANCE OF SAND SAVE FROM BUNKER

NOT ENOUGH CLUB OR BAD MISS-HIT LANDS YOU IN DEEP TROUBLE

▶ Bunkers are a major problem on many holes, but on a treacherous par 3 they're often a secondary hazard. When water threatens the front of the green, seeing your ball finish in sand can almost come as a relief. Several bunkers surrounding the putting surface also accentuate the shape of the green.

Club selection is absolutely crucial on holes like this. Always take plenty of club to give yourself some margin for error – particularly if you're firing at the pin. Play a good tee shot and you fully deserve the birdie chance that awaits you. Even if you unintentionally draw the ball to the left, there's enough carry on the shot to clear the water. Hitting sand is far from disastrous – you still have a reasonable chance to make par.

But if you don't take enough club, or catch the shot a little heavy, your ball is destined for a watery grave. You then have to hole a shot almost as long as your last just to make par – for one loose shot this is a severe punishment.

OPTICAL ILLUSION

PLOT YOUR PROGRESS

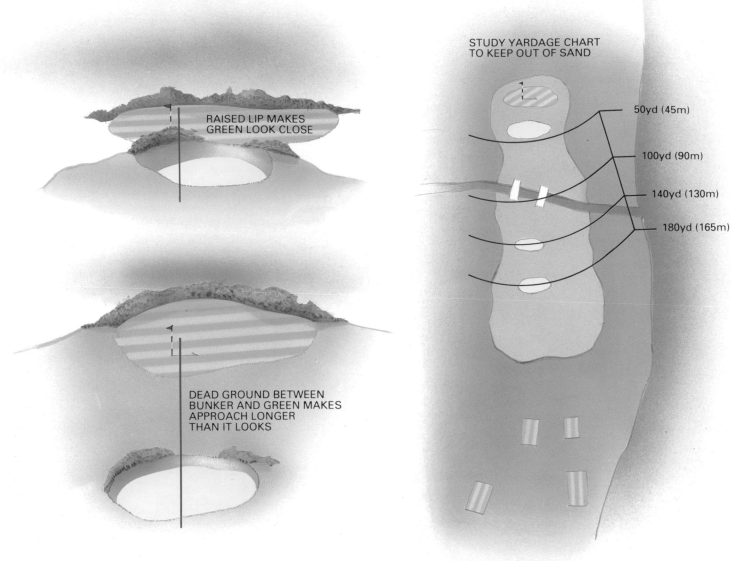

RAISED LIP MAKES GREEN LOOK CLOSE

DEAD GROUND BETWEEN BUNKER AND GREEN MAKES APPROACH LONGER THAN IT LOOKS

STUDY YARDAGE CHART TO KEEP OUT OF SAND

50yd (45m)

100yd (90m)

140yd (130m)

180yd (165m)

Be sure of the shot you want to play before you take your stance. As well as the physical obstacle that bunkers present, they have a nasty habit of playing tricks on the eye. The front lip of a bunker can easily conceal dead ground – particularly if the fairway is flat all the way to the green.

You may think the flag is positioned just over a bunker, when in fact there can be as much as 50yd (45m) of dead ground between the sand and the putting surface. If you're not aware of this, your approach shot is certain to fall short of the mark.

Optical illusions cause nightmares when it comes to club selection. It's the sort of situation where a yardage chart proves invaluable – both off the tee and for your second shot. You can successfully plot your way along the hole, avoiding the traps that lurk up ahead.

On a hole where bunkers scatter the fairway, your mind should immediately turn to accuracy rather than distance. Choose your club wisely – a long shot off grass is usually easier than a shorter one from sand.

For your approach shot, don't be fooled by the dead ground over the bunker. While the eye might tell you it's a 7 iron, try to ignore your instincts. Trust the yardages on the card and choose your club accordingly.

SAND AROUND THE GREENS

Greenside bunkers tend to be positioned around the front half of the putting surface. They're inevitably harder to avoid than fairway bunkers because you have no choice but to flirt with them.

When bunkers eat into one side of a green, caution is the best policy. Aim to pitch your approach shot on the safe half of the green.

This gives you some margin for error should the ball leak to the right or left.

If you need to fly over a bunker to find the green, it's essential to play an attacking stroke. Take plenty of club and imagine the ball pitching on top of the flag – this encourages you not to be short.

You'll soon be pleasantly surprised how often you finish pin high rather than long. And you don't find many bunkers behind

greens, so as long as there's no other trouble at the back, it's better to be long than short.

The biggest mistake you can make is to take too little club and try to force the shot. A heavy handed approach seldom generates the distance you're looking for. You probably find yourself playing your next shot from the bunker in front of the green – which is exactly what you were striving to avoid.

Bunker Recovery Shots

Recovery play from deep greenside bunkers involves a huge variety of trouble shots – no two are likely to be the same. You often need all your wits about you just to find a way out – precise placement is usually the last of your worries.

From time to time all golfers are faced with difficult bunker shots when there seems no escape. Negative thoughts can often crowd the mind – but be firm of purpose. Turn your attention resolutely to the task in hand.

Your first consideration is to try to limit the damage as much as you can. Your thoughts must be on safety – top priority is to avoid playing your next shot from exactly the same spot. Getting up and down in 2 shots isn't the main issue.

Often you can't take a direct

SAFETY FIRST
Bunkers have a nasty habit of testing your technique and imagination to the limit. You may be only a short distance from the green, but try to be realistic. Accept that you can't always aim for the flag from every bunker. Just concentrate on making sure your next shot is from grass and not sand.

UP AND OVER

① OPEN CLUBFACE
From this position you can at least be hopeful of playing for the green but it's no easy task, as the ball needs to travel almost straight up in the air. Align your feet, hips and shoulders left of target with the clubface open.

② WIDE TAKEAWAY
A weak right hand grip helps you keep the clubface open throughout the swing. Take the club away smoothly along the line of your feet and body and break the wrists halfway through the backswing.

pro tip

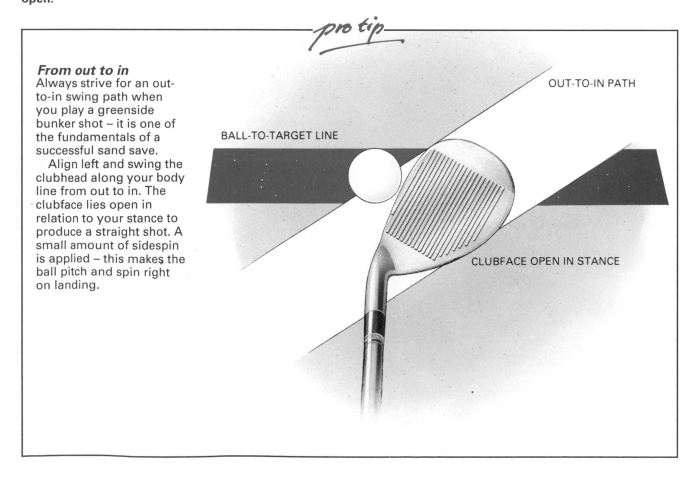

From out to in
Always strive for an out-to-in swing path when you play a greenside bunker shot – it is one of the fundamentals of a successful sand save.

Align left and swing the clubhead along your body line from out to in. The clubface lies open in relation to your stance to produce a straight shot. A small amount of sidespin is applied – this makes the ball pitch and spin right on landing.

OUT-TO-IN PATH

BALL-TO-TARGET LINE

CLUBFACE OPEN IN STANCE

③ FULL BACKSWING
Make a full shoulder turn and allow the club to travel near to horizontal at the top of the backswing. Your whole swing should feel unhurried and under control. Most of your weight is now on the right side.

④ CLUBHEAD SPEED
Your left hand dominates the downswing to set the clubhead traveling on a steep angle of descent. Visualize a spot in the sand behind the ball and imagine the clubhead splashing down on this mark.

⑤ SAND BLAST
Finesse doesn't play a part in this shot – generate as much clubhead speed as possible into impact. The explosion of sand throws the ball vertically into the air, avoiding the face of the bunker.

⑥ HEAD DOWN
The back of the left hand points skyward after impact, preventing the clubface from closing. Sand flying everywhere should help you keep your head down – never be tempted to look up too soon.

ESCAPE SHOT

① NO WAY FORWARD
It's impossible to play a shot at the flag in this situation – the edge of the bunker prevents you from making a backswing or downswing. The only sensible alternative is to play out backwards away from the target.

② FIRM FOOTING
The direction you're hitting the ball means that you can't place both feet in the bunker. Work your right foot well into the sand and flex your left leg. Position most of your weight on your right side.

③ STEEP BACKSWING
Pick the club up quickly on the backswing by breaking the wrists early – this action helps you to swing your arms on the upright plane needed for a high shot. Very little shoulder turn is necessary.

route to the hole so assess the options open to you. Think first of position – you want to make your next shot as easy as possible.

Look around the green and size up the shot carefully. There's nearly always a way out. Don't attempt anything foolhardy – settle instead for playing out sideways or even backwards.

If you're extremely unlucky and you simply can't see a realistic way out, take a penalty drop in the bunker. When the ball is plugged close to the face of the bunker it's better to drop rather than attempt an unlikely escape shot.

Before playing any bunker shot you must consider the texture of the sand. On links and heathland courses the bunker sand is fine and powdery. The clubhead slides through easily so the splash shot is ideal.

Sand on parkland courses tends to be heavy. While most of the bunkers are quite shallow, you still find deep traps eating into the side of some parkland greens. Your clubhead may dig in deep so don't be too delicate. The ball flies lower and runs further than a shot from soft, fine sand.

SAND TACTICS

Once you know in what direction you want to play the ball, think about the techniques required. The high splash shot can help you out of all sorts of trouble – particularly from deep bunkers. A sand wedge is the ideal weapon for the shot.

Adjust your stance to suit the slope of the sand – this is a key to successful recovery. You must put yourself in a balanced position which you can maintain throughout the swing. On an uphill or downhill lie position your shoulders as near to parallel with the sand as is comfortable.

Stand open at address with the clubface aiming square, or slightly open, to your chosen target. Work your feet into the sand to give yourself a solid base. Don't lock your legs rigid – keep them nicely flexed and relaxed. Stiff knees restrict your swing.

Swing high to hit high if the bunker lip in front of you is sizeable. Play the splash shot with authority and accelerate into the sand. You must generate lots of clubhead speed to avoid leaving

the ball in the bunker. Don't worry about hitting too far. The ball travels up as far as it moves forward and you very seldom overshoot the target.

Pick the club up steeply on the backswing by breaking your wrists early. Bring it down sharply on an out-to-in path into the sand – the clubhead cuts under the ball, and the explosion of sand at impact sends the ball almost vertically up in the air.

The forgotten shot
Bunker play is often neglected in practice routines – which doesn't help dispel its reputation as one of the most feared strokes in golf.

But playing off sand isn't all misery. It can be rewarding, particularly in practice. Experiment with shots from different slopes and lies in a variety of bunkers. You build confidence as you understand how to escape from the most difficult situation.

4 **AT THE TOP**
Stop your hands around chest height at the top of the backswing. Your wrists hinge as a result of picking the club up sharply earlier in the swing, and are perfectly positioned to help bring the clubhead down steeply.

5 **PULL DOWN HARD**
The left hand dominates the downswing, pulling the clubhead down hard. Most of your weight should be central – perhaps even a little on the right side. If you sway towards the ball you risk thinning the shot.

6 **SAFELY OUT**
Keep the clubface open as it cuts through the sand under the ball. The back of your left hand should face skyward long after impact. When the shot is played correctly the ball pops high out of the sand to safety.

Resign yourself

When your luck runs out and your ball finishes in a desperate lie, try not to lose heart – one bit of bad luck needn't destroy your round. Don't attempt a miraculous recovery shot – if it doesn't come off you risk taking more strokes in the bunker than you bargained for.

If you're not confident that you can escape at your first attempt, the rules allow you to declare the ball unplayable and take a 1 shot penalty drop. Select a spot that's nearer to the center of the bunker but still within two club lengths of the original position.

Drop the ball at arm's length and shoulder height. Although the ball may be further away from the pin than its original lie, a drop gives you a chance to play for the flag or the edge of the green. You can then comfortably escape from the bunker without disaster.

SAFE ALTERNATIVE

1 OUT OF REACH
A shot at the flag from this situation is possible only off your knees – but this is far too risky to attempt other than in practice. In a competition, simply choose the safest shot that's open to you.

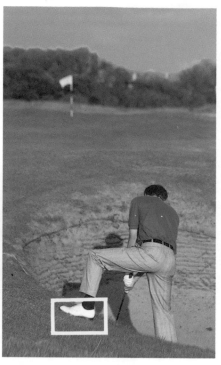

2 SHOOT SIDEWAYS
It's easy to lose your balance with this awkward stance, so anchor your right foot firmly into the sand. Shuffle your left foot until you are comfortable – you must feel stable at address .

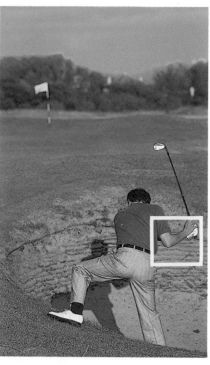

3 HEAD STILL
Break your wrists early and try to keep your right elbow close to your side on the backswing. It's important your head and body are as still as possible – sideways movement causes a thin.

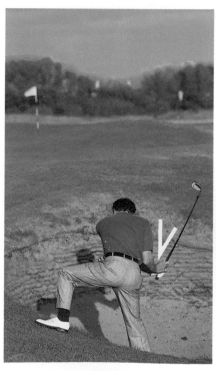

4 ACUTE ANGLE
Pull the bottom of the club down almost vertically with your left hand to create an acute angle between your right arm and the shaft of the club. This action puts the clubhead on a steep angle of descent.

5 RETURN TO ADDRESS
Your left hand should lead the clubhead into the impact area, keeping the clubface open. Aim to strike the sand about a ball's width behind the ball – this guards against the possibility of a thinned shot.

6 SHORT FOLLOWTHROUGH
The splash effect of the sand throws the ball up and out of the bunker. This is one of the few shots where you don't complete your followthrough because the clubhead digs into the edge of the bunker.

Shallow Bunker Shot

In theory the shallow bunker shot should be the easiest stroke there is from sand. There's almost no front lip to negotiate, so height isn't a major consideration. You usually have a choice of shots.

This is certainly true from a shallow fairway bunker – a clean strike is essential but you're free to choose just about any club in the bag, depending on how far you are from the target. However, if the same bunker is close to a green, it often seems to create a problem rather than present an opportunity.

Often you become too tentative – the result is that you fail to escape from shallow bunkers at the

APPROACH WITH AUTHORITY
The shot from a shallow greenside bunker looks so simple – no front lip, perfect lie – that it's easy to think nothing could possibly go wrong. But this shot is only as easy as you make it – you can't afford to be sloppy. Mistakes creep in when you fail to treat the situation with enough care. Play the shot with conviction because you must generate clubhead speed to achieve success out of sand.

✓ THE GREAT ESCAPE

① BALL OPPOSITE LEFT HEEL
Your stance in a shallow greenside bunker should almost be a combination of two different techniques – a splash bunker shot and your standard full swing. Stand with the ball opposite your left heel, align fractionally open to the target and position your weight a little more on the left foot than normal. Even though a high flight is not essential, your sand wedge is still the club best suited to this shot.

② SET IN MOTION
Concentrate on making a smooth one piece takeaway – very much in the way you would with a full shot. This should prevent your wrists breaking too early and helps you take the club along the line of your body. Keep your weight fairly central throughout the backswing – it's dangerous to shift your weight too far either way when you're in a greenside bunker.

③ LONG BACKSWING
You probably seldom need to hit this shot more than 30yd (27m), but it's essential you make an almost full backswing. Note how the shoulders are nicely turned away from the ball – this doesn't vary too much from a normal shot off the fairway. The main difference is that your wrists should hinge a little earlier – this helps create a slightly steeper arc in your swing which promotes the correct angle of attack on the downswing.

4 LATE HIT
One of the major benefits of making a near full backswing is that you can start the downswing in a smooth, unhurried fashion. This gradually generates clubhead speed and helps you coordinate all the moving parts in your swing. Note how pulling the bottom of the club down with the left hand creates an action known as the late hit – this is a key move when you need to strike down and ensures the clubhead doesn't overtake the hands before impact.

5 SPLASH DOWN
Concentrate on a mark about 2in (6cm) behind the ball and imagine the clubhead entering the sand at that point. Stay down through impact – keeping your knees flexed is often an effective way to achieve this. Try to delay the release of your hands for fractionally longer than you would for a full swing – this guards against turning the clubface over too early which often causes the ball to fly to the left.

6 HIGH FLIER
You generate lots of clubhead speed during this swing but look at the early flight of the ball – it's clearly not traveling any great distance. This is the way it should be – the clubhead travels through the sand under the ball rather than inflicting a solid blow. Much about this position resembles a normal followthrough – weight on the left side and the arms pulling your upper body round towards the target.

✗ SWING FAILURE

① ROOM TO IMPROVE
There are no major problems at address, but a few points could be improved upon. Ideally your stance should be a little wider and the feet aligned slightly squarer to the target line.

② GOOD START
The early part of the backswing looks to be in good shape. The arms and the club move in one piece to create the necessary arc away from the ball.

③ COMBINATION OF ERRORS
The shot starts to go seriously wrong at this stage. The club doesn't travel far enough on the backswing, there's an almost complete lack of shoulder turn and the wrists are hinged a little too much. These faults are certain to make it hard for you to generate the necessary clubhead speed through impact.

4 DIGGING DEEP
The poor downswing and disastrous impact position, where far too much sand is taken, are caused by faults that occur earlier in the swing. It's the hopelessly short backswing that causes the panic as you struggle to generate clubhead speed. As is often the case in this situation, the body lunges forward and tempo changes dramatically.

5 DEAD END
This clearly shows that taking too much sand can kill the shot completely. There's plenty of forward movement – head, shoulders, upper body – everything except the ball. Your head coming up too early is a tell-tale sign of anxiety.

6 SADNESS IN SAND
This is one of the most depressing sights in golf – the ball comes down hopelessly short of the target and fails to make a clean break from the sand. While you can take a couple of steps nearer the hole, this does nothing to ease the pain. The next bunker shot is at least as tricky as the last.

pro tip

Lip reading

The most common fault that many golfers commit out of a shallow bunker is leaving the ball in the sand. This is almost certainly the result of being too tentative and failing to accelerate the clubhead through the sand. Because there's no front lip you're easily lulled into a false sense of security.

Playing a positive shot is the most effective cure, but you first need to be in the right frame of mind. Visualize an imaginary lip in front of you to help you achieve this goal.

This sets a more demanding test and forces you mentally to play a positive stroke – one that generates both height and carry – to guarantee you clear the imaginary front lip. Remember, escaping in one should be your first priority.

Once you can combine these qualities with a good feel for distance you have the recipe for success out of any bunker.

first attempt. However, it's important to understand that a shallow bunker shot is no different from most other strokes out of sand. The more you treat it this way, the better you're likely to cope with the shot.

INVISIBLE OBSTACLES

Because there's no physical barrier to overcome in the form of a menacing front lip, your largest obstacle is mental. There's really no short cut to approaching shallow bunker shots in a confident mood. You achieve this by playing them well in practice and then bringing the technique out onto the course with you.

You should always try to play the stroke that involves the least element of chance. The splash bunker shot technique is the one most likely to give you consistently good results.

This method makes the sand work in your favor – one of the keys to good bunker play. You can make a full swing, generate plenty of clubhead speed and yet watch the ball float at no more than a gentle pace towards the flag.

MAJOR MISTAKE

Because very little height is called for, many golfers are tempted to play a chip and run. However, this may be a simple shot from grass, but it's a different story out of a bunker.

Sand can be an unforgiving surface – trying to strike the ball without touching a single grain is extremely difficult. Catch the shot too cleanly and the ball races through the green. Make contact with sand before the ball and your next bunker shot may come a lot sooner than you thought.

Only when there's very little sand in the bunker should you consider playing a chip and run. Your pitching wedge is the best club if you do decide to play it.

PUTTING FROM SAND

Occasionally a putt from a shallow greenside bunker is a clever ploy. Think very carefully before you consider this shot – it's risky and all the conditions need to be heavily stacked in your favor if you're to succeed.

Most importantly, the sand needs to be hard packed and not at all fluffy – this allows the ball to roll relatively smoothly on the surface sand. The lip must also be almost non-existent. Even a ridge of 2in (6cm) – hardly a lip at all on first sight – is probably enough to bring your ball to an abrupt halt.

When you consider whether to putt or not, visualize the front half of the bunker as a ramp. If you can picture the ball rolling up this ramp, and not being stopped by the lip, a putt may well be the right shot. But if there's any doubt in your mind, your sand wedge is ideally suited to getting you out of trouble.

Bunker Close-ups

A sand's eye view of bunker play is the best way to understand and put into practice such well worn phrases as "lifted out on a cushion of sand."

Bunker technique is often shrouded in mystique and approached with fear. But seeing close up what happens at impact cuts through the theory and gets to the heart of sand success.

Once you understand how a ball reacts from sand you can form a clear mental picture of each shot you play.

SPIN BALL WIZARD

From a good greenside bunker lie the clubhead at no time makes contact with the ball. And while there's seldom any great distance between you and the flag, you can easily create backspin if you play a shot correctly.

The action of the clubhead sliding under the ball imparts the spin and sends it high into the air. You can be confident of the ball landing softly, which helps you play a positive stroke.

CONTROL THE SAND STORM
Many professionals would rather be in bunkers than in rough – particularly if the lie is good. They use the sand to help them control the ball – you can do this too if you know what to look for. Confidence out of sand soon filters through to your whole game. Once you can judge precisely how the ball reacts, and the amount of backspin you need (shown by red stripe), you can swing freely on a hole littered with bunkers, relaxed in the knowledge you're able to cope with shots from sand.

SOLVING THE MYSTERY OF SAND

(1) PSYCHOLOGICAL LIFT
There's never a good moment to land in a bunker, but if you find your ball lying well your spirits should immediately be lifted. A good lie means you can accurately judge how the ball behaves. The sand is fine so it's the perfect situation to play the splash bunker shot. Note that the red stripe is vertical at this point.

KEY POINT
Don't ground the club or touch the ball.

(2) **SPLASH DOWN**
The clubhead comes down steeply, cutting into the sand behind the ball. You must accelerate the clubhead into impact, otherwise the sand acts like a barrier, destroying the shot completely. It's the hitting down into the sand that pops the ball up in the air. Although your part in the shot is well under way, the ball is still motionless and the red stripe still vertical.

KEY POINT
Accelerate down smoothly.

3 **BACKSPINNER**
As the clubhead travels down, the ball is lifted up into the air on a blanket of sand. The red line shows clearly the backward rotation of the ball – this is the first sign of spin on the shot that stops the ball quickly on the green. You must play the shot precisely – as contact between clubhead and ball is indirect only total control gives you the spin you require.

KEY POINT
Feel the club sliding down and under the ball.

(4) **SAND BLAST**
The explosion effect of the sand is clear to see as the ball is propelled upwards and forwards. The wide, rounded sole helps keep the clubhead sliding through the sand underneath the ball. At this stage the ball is behind the clubhead and has rotated backwards 1½ times. It's important the clubface points at the target through impact for as long as possible.

KEY POINT
Keep up clubhead momentum.

5 HEADING FOR SAFETY
The clubhead leaves a shallow trough in the sand as the ball floats towards the target. The shot is played firmly and with authority – yet a soft landing on the green combined with backspin ensure the ball runs very little.

Practice makes perfect
If you usually take a practice swing before every shot, do the same when you prepare to play out of a bunker. Remember, the rules say you can't touch the sand with the club so stand outside the bunker and practice the swing you intend making. This helps give a feel for the shot – once in the sand you find you're more comfortable over the ball.

Downhill Bunker Shots

The downhill bunker shot – when the ball ends on the downslope – is one of the most awkward and feared sand shots to play. This lie occurs when the ball trickles into a bunker without enough power to run down to the bottom.

With any bunker shot it's important to hit the sand first. But with a downhill lie the downslope and lip of the bunker make hitting sand difficult. Practice the technique to avoid taking a penalty or playing backwards out of the bunker.

YOUR SET-UP

You might not be able to get into the bunker with both feet to take up your normal set-up – you may have to play with one foot on the fairway.

This position makes your upper body tilt in the direction of the slope. Though it's awkward and uncomfortable, practicing from this angle helps develop your downhill technique.

If you're really unlucky with the lie of the ball you won't be able to get into the bunker at all. In this situation you have to bend down on one knee – or perhaps both – and play the shot as normally as you can. Get as comfortable as possible, and be positive about your stroke.

Keep your clubface open as for a normal bunker shot but bear in mind that the ball may fly lower from this type of lie.

Check the sand
Sand texture is important for a good splash out from a downhill bunker shot.

If the sand is soft and deep rather than wet and compact the shot is much easier – with wet, shallow sand there's a danger the clubhead won't slide under the ball. The shot may come out low with a lot of roll. Use a narrow-soled sand wedge to reduce the chance of a bounce, and be positive – hit firmly and with confidence.

KEEP YOUR HANDS AHEAD
At address your hands are ahead of the club – hold this position throughout the stroke to steepen your angle of attack into the sand.

BALANCE YOURSELF
A downhill bunker shot is made more difficult if you can't get both feet into the bunker. Lean forward from the waist to keep your balance. Your feet should be aligned left of target – an open clubface compensates. Position the ball further back in your stance than for normal bunker play to ensure that you take sand with the stroke.

ADDRESS AND ATTACK

(1) **GET COMFORTABLE**
Open your stance and your clubface. You probably need to shuffle about a bit and rehearse the backswing to make certain you miss the back lip of the bunker when you start the swing.

THE SWING

Whatever way you have to tackle the shot, exaggerate the wrist break at the start of the swing so you pick up the club more acutely and avoid touching the bunker lip. This action also steepens your angle of attack which helps you hit into the sand behind the ball.

The quick wrist break moves your hands ahead of the clubface. Keep this position as you swing down and through the sand – have your right hand underneath the shaft as you strike through.

With your throughswing make a conscious effort to swing down and through the slope. This should be quite easy as you'll be leaning in the correct direction.

TRIAL AND ERROR

The downhill bunker shot is very much a feel shot – how the ball lies is a critical factor. Try shuffling back and forth to get comfortable. Experiment with how much you open the clubface at address and how acutely you break your wrists to start the swing.

Forget about reaching a respectable distance – be grateful to get out and hope for a good putt.

(2) **BACKSWING**
Because of the acute angle of your upper body at address, you must pick up your club steeply to clear the back lip. Your open body position means you swing the club slightly outside the ball-to-target line.

Alliss' natural ability
Peter Alliss – the all-around player and British TV commentator – shows his skill at tackling the downhill bunker shot. Very much a feel player, Alliss was able to attack the sand and lift the ball neatly out. Note how far back the ball is positioned to allow for the steep slope.

(3) **LEAD WITH HANDS**
Let your hands lead the clubhead so that the face is open on contact with the sand. Don't be tempted to look up too early to see where the ball is going – your head movement could destroy the shot.

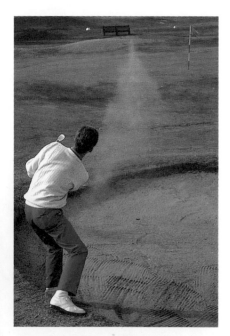

(4) **THROUGHSWING**
Keep your right hand underneath the shaft as you swing through. The ball is thrown out by the sheer force of the clubhead hitting the sand underneath and behind the ball. Don't be too ambitious – be content simply to get out of the bunker from this difficult lie.

pro tip

Polished sand play

GO TO BOARDING SCHOOL
The mid range bunker shot – one of 25-60yd (23-55m) – is an awkward stroke for any level of player. However, one drill helps you to fine tune the correct technique, and become a confident and proficient performer from this tricky distance.

Because crisp striking is essential to gauge the weight of the shot correctly, you need to nip the ball cleanly off the sand. To practice clipping the ball crisply, lay down a wooden board about 45yd (41m) from the practice green – or play to an umbrella stuck in the ground. It doesn't have to be in a trap, but practicing with your feet in sand is realistic.

Place the ball in the center of your stance and align parallel to the target line – not left like a greenside bunker shot. You may want to play the shot with a pitching wedge to lessen the chance of bouncing the blade into the back of the ball. The longer distances are also easier to judge with a pitching wedge.

Concentrate on swinging with a smooth, easy rhythm, and attack the ball from a steeper angle than you would for a greenside sand shot. This ensures you catch the ball first and not the board. The ball flies out on a good trajectory with plenty of backspin. Clipping the wood first results in a duff or thin. Let the club do the work – don't try to lift the ball up.

If you can strike consistently well flighted pitches from such a hard and bare lie, you should have no problem nipping a ball off sand without fatting or thinning the shot. This improves your mid range bunker accuracy enormously and boosts your sand save percentages.

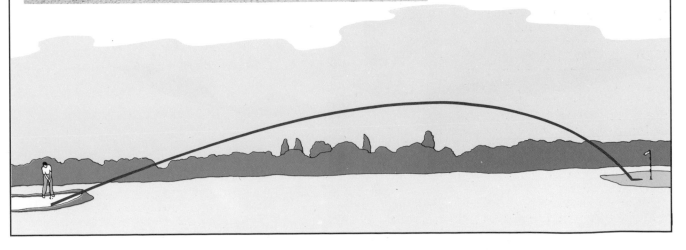

SLIDING UNDER

The blade of your sand wedge must slide under the ball to hit a controlled splash shot out of a greenside trap. You have to take sand, but it must be just the right amount. Too little and you're in danger of thinning the ball, too much and you fluff the ball.

Ideally you should aim to start taking sand about 1 in (4cm) behind the ball. The blade should continue through impact on a shallow path floating the ball out on a blanket of sand.

To perfect this technique, try either the tee peg or double ball drill.

TEE PEG DRILL

Push a tee peg into the sand 1in (2.5cm) behind the ball. Forget about the ball – concentrate only on the tee. Be sure you set up properly and then make your swing. Aim to scoop out the tee peg with a sliding action by hitting slightly behind it – so you contact the sand at the critical 1½ (4cm) behind the ball.

If you have made the correct shape of swing the ball should naturally pop up into the air without you having to think about it. You can take this technique out on to the course by picking a spot behind the ball to aim at. Don't look at the back of the ball.

DOUBLE BALL DRILL

Another way to achieve the same effect is to try to splash two balls out with the same stroke. Place one ball directly behind another pointing at the target. Set up imagining the ball nearest the hole to be your target ball, but don't aim to hit it. Try to slide your blade under both balls.

Having to go under the first ball to be able to splash the target ball out naturally ingrains the correct technique into your muscle memory.

It's best to practice in a low-lipped trap – the target ball does not fly out as high as you would expect because it is bumped forward by the first ball. Keep your eye on the first ball as it lofts daintily out of the trap – this gives you a good idea how the target ball will behave when you use the same technique with only one ball.

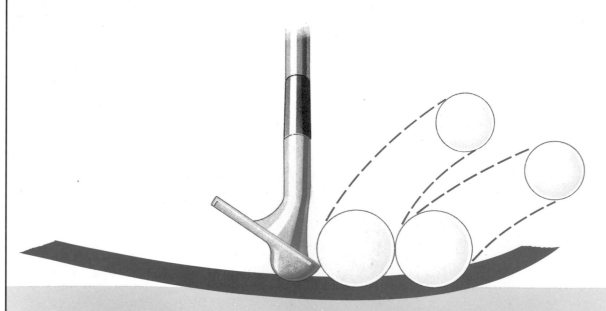

SLIDE BLADE UNDER TWO BALLS
FOR CORRECT SPLASH TECHNIQUE

Subtly Shaped Driver

Having the know-how and ability to shape shots is a wonderful asset to your game. Though most golfers only try to shape their irons – particularly on approaches – there is huge scope to maneuver your driver as well.

Usually amateurs who do try to shape their drivers only attempt it on a dog-leg – to hug the contours of the hole. But a faint draw or fade from the tee is useful for far more than just that.

Safe shots, finding extra distance and playing for position are all made easier by a subtle shaping of your driver. On a tightish but long hole – where you need length and accuracy – a gentle fade is the shot to hit. Starting down the left side slightly, the ball drifts back to the center of the fairway and lands softly – thanks to a higher flight with more backspin than normal.

A draw is less controllable but produces greater roll and length than a fade – because of the drawspin. This flight is extremely handy for squeezing that extra bit of yardage out of a drive – perhaps when you think a par 5 may be in range in 2.

Both shapes are well suited for positional play. You can avoid trouble on one side of the hole by moving the ball away from it. And by maneuvering a shot to one half of the fairway or other, you can leave yourself a better line into the flag.

Don't be fooled into thinking that you have to make drastic set-up changes to shape a driver. If you do, your intended faint fade turns into a carve and your draw into a big hook. Subtle shaping needs subtle changes – as the straight face of a driver accentuates any sideways movement and exaggerates its effect.

PLAYING FOR POSITION
Thinking ahead is vital if you're to make scoring easier for yourself. When you stand on a tee, look down the hole and work out where best to place your ball for your approach. If you need to hit the ball down the left side to give yourself a better line into the flag – as at the 1st at Valderrama – shaping your driver could be the answer. If you aim down the center of the hole and play a slight draw, you're almost guaranteed to finish down the left side. At worst you should be in the middle of the fairway if the shot doesn't quite come off.

FRACTIONALLY OPEN FOR GENTLE FADE

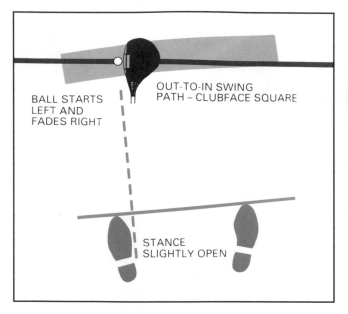

BALL STARTS LEFT AND FADES RIGHT

OUT-TO-IN SWING PATH – CLUBFACE SQUARE

STANCE SLIGHTLY OPEN

ALIGN LEFT, AIM SQUARE
To hit the subtle left to righter you only need to change your normal set-up by the tiniest amount. You must still square up the clubface with the center of the fairway – or the line on which you want the ball to end up – but you must stand a fraction open. It's a matter of an inch or two – any more and the fade can get away from you.

OUTSIDE ATTACK
Forget about your set-up and solely concentrate on swinging as normal – along the line of your feet. You naturally swing slightly outside the target line to the top and then attack the ball from out to in – even though your swing plane in relation to your body is normal.

TELL-TALE THROUGHSWING
As you swing through back on the inside there is a natural tendency to stop your hands releasing as quickly as normal. This is no bad thing as it helps the fading flight, but you must never hold it for too long – or the fade turns into a slice. The high-handed, slight flourish into the finish is a tell-tale sign of the fade.

FAINT DRAWING TECHNIQUE

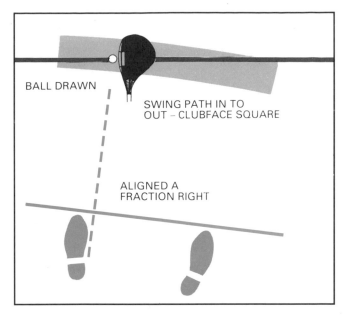

BALL DRAWN

SWING PATH IN TO
OUT – CLUBFACE SQUARE

ALIGNED A
FRACTION RIGHT

ALIGN RIGHT, AIM SQUARE

You probably need to change your set-up less to play the draw than you do for the fade. If you're not careful it is easy for the shot to be overdone as the ball flies lower with drawspin and runs on landing. Align only a fraction right but keep your blade exactly square. Position the ball as normal – opposite your left heel.

POINTING RIGHT AT TOP

Swing along your normal plane – resist the temptation to take the club back too much on the inside in an attempt to promote the draw. If you move into your usual top of the backswing position, your driver shaft should be pointing slightly right of target.

NATURAL INSIDE ATTACK

If you swing down at the ball from slightly on the inside as usual, the angle of attack is accentuated. Even though you have dropped the club down into impact in your normal way, the actual path in relation to the target line is from in to out due to your alignment. With the blade square, the ball starts down the right side and drifts back to the center of the fairway.

Maneuvering Mark

There is such a variety of layouts around the world that you must be able to shape the ball well to become a top flight performer. Not only can it get you out of trouble but it can give you the edge over your fellow competitors.

Mark James has that ability. Although his action is slightly unconventional his understanding of the technique is excellent and he has superb control through the ball. The five time Ryder Cup player is equally at home with hitting a fade or a draw, and has used this prowess to great effect when tackling the courses on the Euro Tour.

The sweeping, tree-lined holes at Woburn – home of the Dunhill British Masters – demand subtly shaped drives if you're to conquer the course. Mark certainly used his maneuvering skills there in 1990 when he won by 2 shots from David Feherty.

Height for flight

Shaping the driver doesn't just mean moving the ball sideways, you can also flight shots at different heights to suit your purposes.

If you want to keep the ball lower than normal – perhaps to combat the wind – try teeing the ball slightly higher than you usually do.

This helps you create a more sweeping action and attack the ball on a shallower angle than normal. Instead of catching the ball on the up, you should strike the ball on a more level plane and drive the ball forward under the wind.

Teeing the ball up also helps you to hit the ball higher if you position the ball forward in your stance – useful to gain distance downwind. Because the ball is forward in the stance the clubhead attacks it more on the up and so sends the shot on a higher flight than normal.

Knocking an iron into shape

Although shaping a driver is great for your game, there are times when you should be wary of hitting it. As stressed by all teachers, any change in your driver set-up that isn't only a fraction away from your norm can be dangerous.

Because a driver's face is so straight, it is all too easy to overcook your intended shape. So when you're faced with a curving dog-leg hole – where you need to move the ball quite a lot to keep it on the fairway – it is unwise to hit a driver.

If you try to maneuver the ball too much, just a slight loss of control sends your ball flying away into trouble. Your best option is to hit a long iron. A 1 iron has a shorter shaft and a more lofted face than a driver, making it easier to control. But it still hits the ball a good distance and has a steep enough face to shape the ball markedly.

But beware of hitting a big draw with a 1 iron. The blade – though still square to the target line – is delofted at address, and your draw may become a hook. Go with a 3 or 4 iron instead – they take on the loft of a longer iron.

Beat Driver Phobia

Those who dread the driver and steer clear of the club at all costs are missing out on one of the most uplifting experiences in golf – a good bash with a driver bites a large chunk out of most holes and is a tremendous boost to your confidence.

The problem for a lot of golfers is not always genuine fear of hitting this club, more a case of struggling to find a driver they feel comfortable with.

If you've ever felt this way you probably take the headcover off your driver very reluctantly. It's hardly surprising that some golfers store their drivers in the cupboard rather than the golf bag.

The search for that elusive longest club in the bag is rather like looking for your perfect putter – it often takes time and can easily mean experimenting with several makes and styles.

The driver is a very personal club – far more so than any set of irons you'll ever buy. Once you find one you like, stick with it through thick and thin. The club takes on a far less frightening appearance and at times you're likely to feel you can hit almost any shot – this is very important in a pressure situation.

DRIVING LESSON

Even with a club that suits you it's important to know how to drive before you can stand on the tee with total confidence.

Although it's mainly a distance club, never hit your driver flat out unless the situation is really desperate and crying out for you to take a gamble.

The well known phrase that you

TAKE THE EASY OPTION
Every golfer drives the ball badly from time to time – even the best in the world. Don't feel you have to slog your way through a slump with your driver – if you're suffering from a bout of low confidence it could take a depressingly long time. Move down to your 3 wood and swing the club just as you would a driver. You don't lose much distance, the club is easier to hit, and an upturn in morale is just round the corner.

SUBSTITUTE DRIVER

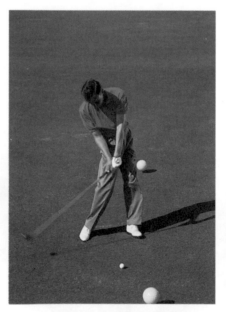

① FIRM FOUNDATION
The 3 wood is much easier to hit than the driver and gives you almost as much distance, so if you're struggling off the tee, a more lofted wood is often the short term answer. Adopt exactly the same address position as you would for a driver – the only adjustment you need to make is teeing the ball fractionally lower to allow for the smaller clubhead.

② FIRST STEP
Try to ensure that your first movement away from the ball is correct. Sweep the club back close to the ground for at least 12in (30cm). This serves a dual purpose – it prevents your wrists breaking too early and sets the club on a wide arc away from the ball. Both are essential for generating clubhead speed during the swing.

③ HINGE POINT
The importance of creating a wide arc is clear at this stage of the swing, as the left side is pulled into perfect position. The right leg acts as a brace supporting more than half your body weight. At about the time your right arm folds your wrists should begin to hinge – this helps ensure the clubhead travels on a consistent plane to the top.

④ ROCK SOLID
The top of the backswing is one of the most crucial stages of the swing, whichever club is in your hands. Look out for certain essential points – full shoulder turn; hips rotated about 45° from address; shaft of the club as close to horizontal as possible; and good weight transfer away from the ball.

⑤ NATURAL PROGRESSION
The downswing is made that much easier when you work hard at getting your backswing right. The solid pose achieved at the top helps trigger the correct moves into impact. The body unwinds from a coiled position and the weight shifts onto the left side – each combines to generate clubhead speed.

⑥ TURN FOR THE BETTER
This fluid followthrough is the result of swinging correctly – you can't put yourself in a good position through the ball if you make mistakes earlier. Once you start to strike your 3 wood well, move up to your driver – you stand a better chance of hitting good shots with this club when your confidence is high.

CARDINAL POINTS

Many courses have practice greens that aren't big enough to hit a full driver. For many golfers the local driving range presents the only opportunity to practice with this club. If you're among this group of golfers, you must be aware of some helpful points to ensure you make constructive use of your time and money.

Most importantly you need to avoid the greatest temptation of all, which is to mindlessly thrash away as if you were in a long driving contest. You see this at every range with "aerosol golfers" spraying the ball to all points of the compass. It seems like a good idea – after all, knocking the ball a long way is fun and there's a full bucket of balls waiting to be hit – but this activity has a damaging effect on your game.

Swing within yourself and always take your time between drives. Never hit too many shots – about 20 or so is an ideal number. Only pull out the driver towards the end of a practice session and never at the beginning – you need to be properly warmed up to hit the ball well with this club.

You also have to accept that concentration can be hard at times when you're at a crowded driving range. With balls shooting from the bays like tracer bullets it's easy to get distracted. Try to ignore the blur of activity going on around you and look at it as good experience – if you can focus at a driving range you shouldn't have problems doing so on the course.

Bear in mind that the balls at a golf range are usually quite poor quality. They feel soft off the clubface and don't travel as far as the type you would use on the course. So don't feel miffed if your best drive falls well short of the usual mark. Another drawback of most golf ranges is the fixed rubber tees. If they're at a different height to those you're used to, don't hit balls off them. It's bound to feel strange and you may find yourself making adjustments to your swing. Use tee pegs if possible – otherwise don't hit drives at all.

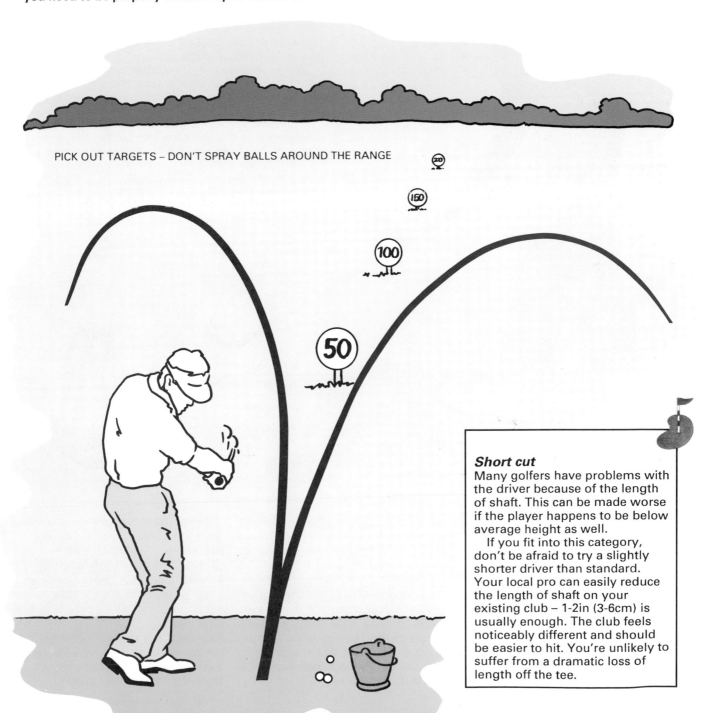

PICK OUT TARGETS – DON'T SPRAY BALLS AROUND THE RANGE

Short cut
Many golfers have problems with the driver because of the length of shaft. This can be made worse if the player happens to be below average height as well.

If you fit into this category, don't be afraid to try a slightly shorter driver than standard. Your local pro can easily reduce the length of shaft on your existing club – 1-2in (3-6cm) is usually enough. The club feels noticeably different and should be easier to hit. You're unlikely to suffer from a dramatic loss of length off the tee.

pro tip

TWO UMBRELLAS AT DRIVER DISTANCE

30yd (27m) APART – WIDTH OF AVERAGE FAIRWAY

Realistic aim

When you practice with your driver it's important you set yourself a realistic target to hit. Two umbrellas serve the purpose as well as anything. Stick them in the ground at the distance you hit your driver – about 30yd (27m) apart represents the width of the average fairway.

You're unlikely to hit every ball between the umbrellas, but the target at least gives you the sort of landing area you would expect to find on the course. If you're driving well you can achieve a good success rate and gradually build on your confidence. If you don't have two umbrellas, aim between two trees at the end – this is an equally realistic target area.

Whatever you do, don't try to pump drives at a lone pencil-thin tree in the distance. This is likely to destroy what confidence you started the day with because it's such a difficult target to hit.

TAKE YOUR TIME – SWING WITHIN YOURSELF

should swing your driver as you do a 9 iron is one of the finest single pieces of advice you can absorb.

Try to feel as though you're swinging at about 70% of full power. This gives you the distance you need and, more importantly, the control which is essential for consistently finding the fairway.

When you stand on the tee it's important to do all you can to put yourself in a positive frame of mind – how you feel over the ball makes all the difference between success and misery.

Remember, hit a good drive away and you're rewarded with a much shorter approach than if you were to play safe with a more lofted club. This is a far better mental attitude than worrying whether or not you can keep the ball out of the trees.

Other positive points are also worth drawing upon if you suffer problems with the driver:

❍ Tee the ball high enough to ensure that the ground doesn't even come into play – this helps eliminate the risk of catching the shot heavy.

❍ Select the perfect spot on the teeing area so that you have an even patch of ground and a good foundation for your swing.

Develop the Power Hit

Millions of golfers throughout the world constantly strive for more power and extra distance. Too many fail and become wild because they try to swing faster to gain more length.

Greater swing speed does not equal greater distance. Clubhead speed is the critical factor. This is generated by a combination of dynamic body action and fast hands. For maximum power you need to create a lag of the clubhead behind your hands on the downswing, and release into impact at the last possible moment – the late hit.

The world's most powerful golfers are all natural late hitters and have no need to force the hands to work. But luckily you can develop this power hit to a degree – without ruining your tempo, rhythm and control.

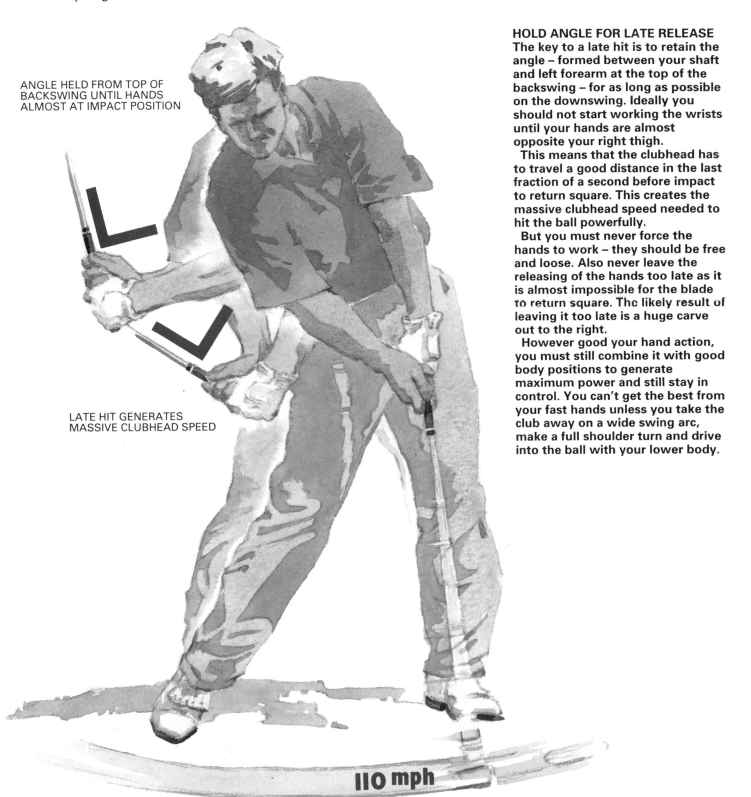

ANGLE HELD FROM TOP OF BACKSWING UNTIL HANDS ALMOST AT IMPACT POSITION

LATE HIT GENERATES MASSIVE CLUBHEAD SPEED

110 mph

HOLD ANGLE FOR LATE RELEASE
The key to a late hit is to retain the angle – formed between your shaft and left forearm at the top of the backswing – for as long as possible on the downswing. Ideally you should not start working the wrists until your hands are almost opposite your right thigh.

This means that the clubhead has to travel a good distance in the last fraction of a second before impact to return square. This creates the massive clubhead speed needed to hit the ball powerfully.

But you must never force the hands to work – they should be free and loose. Also never leave the releasing of the hands too late as it is almost impossible for the blade to return square. The likely result of leaving it too late is a huge carve out to the right.

However good your hand action, you must still combine it with good body positions to generate maximum power and still stay in control. You can't get the best from your fast hands unless you take the club away on a wide swing arc, make a full shoulder turn and drive into the ball with your lower body.

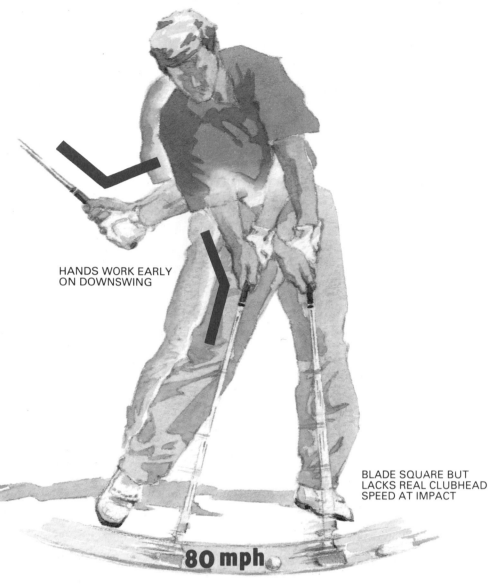

HANDS WORK EARLY
ON DOWNSWING

BLADE SQUARE BUT
LACKS REAL CLUBHEAD
SPEED AT IMPACT

80 mph

THE SWING OF A MERE MORTAL
Most decent golfers have an element of the late hit in their swings. But most just fail to get maximum power out of their action because their hands and wrists start working into impact a fraction before the ideal point. There is nothing wrong with this action – in fact it is easier to control than a very late hitter's – but you can improve it slightly through practice.

pro tip

Power drills

Although it is difficult to teach the late hit to someone who doesn't naturally have good hands, it is still possible to develop it to some degree by using drills.

○ **Downswing hold.** One simple drill helps you ingrain the feeling of the correct late hitter's downswing action into your muscle memory. Set up as normal and take a short iron to the top. Then start down concentrating on holding your wrists firm. Swing down to a point when your hands are almost opposite your right thigh. Stop.

Only hold it there for a fraction of a second – so you don't lose your rhythm – then move the club back to the top and repeat three times without ever unhinging your wrists. On the third swing continue past the stopping point and release your hands into the ball.

Keep repeating this drill. You should soon feel yourself creating a little more lag and power. Don't worry if you push the balls slightly to start with – in time you should naturally work your hands more, so that the blade returns square at impact.

○ **Bell ringer.** Many teaching professionals suggest using your imagination to help develop the power hit. Think of yourself pulling down hard on a bell rope from the top of the backswing. This action of trying to ring a bell automatically makes your hands pull sharply down and keeps your wrists from working too soon on helping you produce the late hit.

masterclass

Mighty Fred

If there is one golfer in the world today who perfectly illustrates the mix of an easy swing with awesome power, it has to be Fred "Boom Boom" Couples. The distances he smacks the ball are often unbelievable, because his swing is so languid, smooth and unhurried.

The slow tempo belies the fact that Fred's hands start working into impact extremely late, and so generate enormous clubhead speed. The lag he creates is astonishing, and even when his hands are almost at their impact position, the clubhead trails way behind.

This action comes naturally and Fred never forces the shot. This means he has control to go with his might – a potent combination that has lifted Couples into the world's top rank.

Lanny Wadkins: King of the Fairway Wood

Forget about the armchair pundits, when your fellow pros vote you the best fairway wood player on tour it really means you're the best. That is exactly what the US Tour golfers have said about the seven time Ryder Cup star Lanny Wadkins for years.

Renowned for his no-nonsense approach and magical matchplay abilities, no opponent can ever take Lanny for granted. No one can afford to be complacent after finding the green from long range, if Wadkins is 230yd (210m) away with his 4 wood in hand. He can lay one in there with ease and leave them scrambling for a half.

SWISH HITTER

His fast-hitting, attacking style wins many admirers, but the flurry of wood and steel is not just an aggressive swipe – there is method in his action. The "fastest gun in the west" – a nickname coined because of his speedy approach to the game – is slightly unorthodox, but bases his superb hitting on sound fundamentals.

Lanny's shot visualization and striking are the most impressive parts of his fairway wood play, and every golfer can learn from his method.

By subtly changing his set-up and swing the burly Virginian manufactures exquisite strokes. Whether it's a low, drilling wind cheater or a high, soft-landing floater, Lanny knows the exact technique needed to bring it off.

He takes time to size up the stroke, thinking of the shape of shot he needs and the set-up and swing to produce it. But after careful thought he is quick to get into position and fire the ball away – he never dwells.

GET SET UP, GO

As long as you visualize the shot carefully before you play, there is no need to take time over the stroke. Like Lanny, walk into position, set up and then go for it. If your swing thoughts are correct for the shape of shot you need, only doubts can creep in if you loiter over the ball.

But striking the ball quite quickly after setting up doesn't mean you have to swing fast as well. Though Lanny has a quick tempo, his rhythm is good and he keeps himself under control throughout the swing.

POWER FADE PERFECTION

①SMART SET-UP
Once decided on hitting his stock fairway wood shot – the high power fade – Wadkins moves quickly into position. With the blade square to the target and his feet, hips and shoulders slightly open, Lanny looks relaxed and ready to go.

②POWER EXTENSION
The extension on the takeaway is enormous. His left arm is still perfectly straight, and this creates a very wide swing arc. His legs are active and he has already turned his shoulders a good deal. All of Lanny's backswing moves are designed to produce power.

③TOP MODEL
A powerful action is no good unless your club swings on line. Lanny completes his massive shoulder-turning backswing on perfect plane. There is no hint of an arched or cupped left wrist, which means the clubface is square at the top. If you move into a coiled position like Lanny's, you have a great base to swing down into impact on the correct path.

(4) DYNAMICALLY DOWN
From the top, Lanny drops his hands down forcefully towards the ball leaving his clubhead trailing way behind. Instead of flailing his arms uncontrollably to the outside – as many amateurs do when they swing aggressively – he controls the slight out-to-in path by keeping his right arm tucked in.

(5) EXACTING STRIKE
Fast hands enable Lanny to return the blade square. Combined with an excellent drive of his legs into and through impact they create a huge amount of power. His balance and clubhead control are so good throughout the swing that he strikes the ball sweetly and true. A full release of the hands through impact is also essential for control.

(6) FLOWING AND STABLE
Lanny stays superbly balanced on his full and flowing throughswing. Staying with the shot – keeping the head behind the ball through impact – ensures that all the good moves on the backswing and downswing aren't wasted by rising off the shot.

(7) HIGH HANDS, HIGH BALL
Because Lanny maintains a good rhythm, strikes fractionally down on the shot and swings on a slightly out-to-in path, the ball starts a fraction left of target and rises high. These traits are all essential to hit a controlled, left-to-right, soft-landing wood.

Driver off the Fairway

The driver off the fairway is an extremely effective weapon when used in the correct way. But it should only be played when you can gain a definite advantage.

The shot produces a low-boring trajectory – ideal when hitting into wind, or for a long running ball to a distant target – but it's also difficult to play perfectly. Only advanced players should attempt this shot – it's not for high handicappers.

WEIGH UP THE RISKS

Use the shot to reach a long par 4 into the wind or to get home in 2 on a par 5. Yet if there is only a small chance of success and trouble looms near the green, it's wiser to play a long iron and then

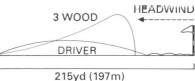
THOUGHT AND TEMPO
The secret of success is positive and careful thinking, while maintaining good rhythm with a normal swing. With the feet slightly open the ball starts fractionally left and slides back to the right during flight. The ball flies low and can run long distances, perfect for playing into wind.

hit a short iron in.

The lie must be flat or slightly uphill – to act as a launching pad – and the ball must be sitting well, preferably on dry ground. When the ball is lying badly always think hard about hitting the shot even if there is a chance of reaching the green. It's a tricky enough shot to play well without added problems.

Many regard the driver off the fairway as the hardest of all shots, but as long as the lie is good the risks are mainly in the mind. The fact that most good golfers happily hit a 3 wood off the fairway makes their fear all the more unnecessary.

There is only a slight difference in the degree of loft, the center of gravity and length of shaft from a 3 wood to a driver. The driver is just a bit more difficult to play.

THE TECHNIQUE

The basic technique of hitting the driver from the fairway is the same as from a tee peg. At address, position the ball opposite or slightly in front of your left heel and aim the clubface at the target as normal.

Your feet should be fractionally open – this slightly increases the loft on the driver to help get the ball airborne and to guard against the snap hook. Because you are aligning slightly left and your clubface is square, the ball starts left and moves gently to the right in the flight.

Think positively – imagine you are hitting a 3 wood – and swing as normal. Don't overhit the ball – rhythm is far more important when applying power.

The key difference between hitting off the fairway and from a tee peg is timing. It needs to be perfect to achieve good results from the fairway. It's important to strike the ball at the bottom of your swing arc, and to sweep it off the turf.

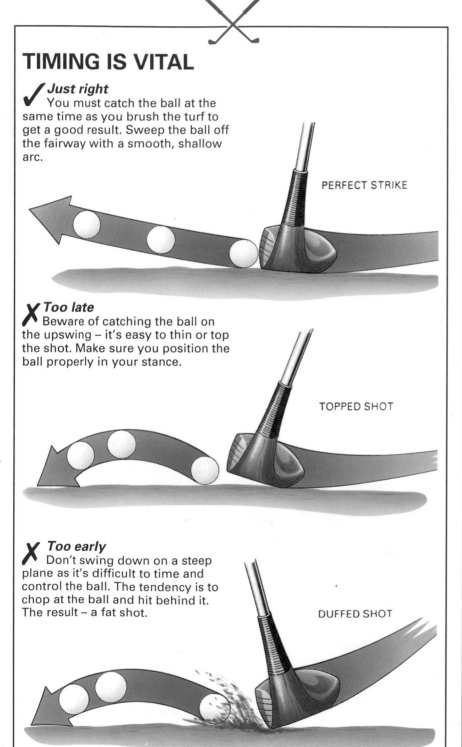

TIMING IS VITAL

✓ *Just right*
You must catch the ball at the same time as you brush the turf to get a good result. Sweep the ball off the fairway with a smooth, shallow arc.

PERFECT STRIKE

✗ *Too late*
Beware of catching the ball on the upswing – it's easy to thin or top the shot. Make sure you position the ball properly in your stance.

TOPPED SHOT

✗ *Too early*
Don't swing down on a steep plane as it's difficult to time and control the ball. The tendency is to chop at the ball and hit behind it. The result – a fat shot.

DUFFED SHOT

Ian's killer blow
The driver from the fairway presents Ian Woosnam with few problems because he is such a great timer of the ball. Combined with his power he can reach greens that are out of range for most golfers.

In the 1989 Irish Open at Portmarnock, the little Welshman came to the 514yd par-5 16th neck and neck with Philip Walton. But Woosie struck two drivers one after the other – the second off the fairway – to within 15ft (5m) of the hole to make birdie. He went on to win the title.

Tight Drives

Every golfer goes through it – a dreaded fear of driving down narrow fairways. Seeing a tight, tree-lined hole or a hummocked fairway flanked by pot bunkers and heavy rough can be a daunting experience.

A poor mental state is the main culprit for finding trouble down an unforgiving hole, as it badly affects your swing. A nervous disposition tightens the golfing muscles and your action can become abrupt and stiff.

FREE STYLE

Trying to guide the ball off the tee is disastrous. Strive to swing freely with rhythm and make sure you release through the ball – both essential for accurate hitting.

Many players are under the illusion that to find the fairway they must aim smack down the middle and hit a ripper that bisects the hole. But a shaped shot is usually your best asset in finding the short stuff.

By aiming down one side of the fairway and hitting either a fade or draw, you almost double the effective landing area. As a general rule the fade aimed down the left side is the safer stroke of the two, as the ball lands softer than a drawn shot.

Because you must always play away from trouble, be open minded which shape you hit. The severity of the trouble either side of the fairway determines your tee shot.

If there's trouble of equal danger both sides of the hole, play the fade – unless the fairway slopes from left to right. In that case a draw is best to hold the ball on the hill.

DOUBLE TROUBLE

If one side of the fairway is more punishing than the other, play toward the lesser danger – even if it means hitting a draw. It may sound ludicrous, but even if your ball rolls into water on one side it may well be better than the fate on the other side – perhaps out of bounds.

Positioning yourself on the tee correctly also helps you to stay out of trouble. Tee up on the side of the worst trouble so it's easier to hit away from it.

Driving safely down a tight hole isn't just a matter of shaping the ball with a free and easy action – club selection is also vital.

An iron is a safer club than a wood and should be easier to hit the fairway with. Look at the overall yardage of the hole. If you can

CAREFREE DRIVING
Don't be intimidated by a narrow, tree-lined fairway. Try giving your driver a rip to develop a confident, go-getter attitude. Standing up there and letting fly helps you to swing freely and release properly. Finding the fairway with a wood is so satisfying that it boosts your mental state, and should help to cure any timidity.

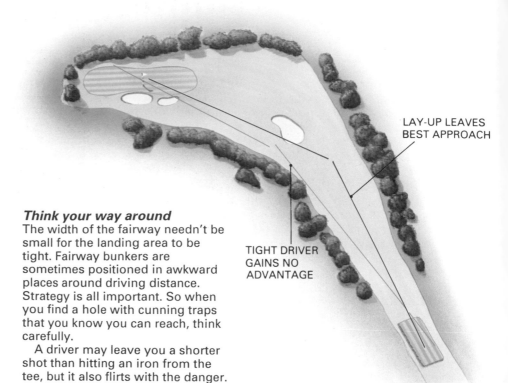

HOOK STILL IN PLAY

DRAW AWAY FROM WORST TROUBLE IS SAFEST SHOT

DANGEROUS FADE

LAY-UP LEAVES BEST APPROACH

TIGHT DRIVER GAINS NO ADVANTAGE

Safe shapes

Hitting down one side of the fairway and moving the ball back toward the middle gives you extra margin for error. Even though a fade is the safest shot, sometimes a draw is the one to play. When an out of bounds fence runs down the right side and trees down the left, play a draw.

The punishment for going OB is worse than overdoing the draw and bounding into the trees. You have to play 3 off the tee for going over the fence but you still have a shot on in the woods. If you're lucky you may have a clear passage to the green, but even settling for a chip out sideways is better than having to reload from the tee.

afford to hit an iron on a par 4 and still reach the green with your next, do so. And if you're certain you can't reach a par 5 in 2, play an iron from the tee to be safe and ensure a good second.

For any tee shot on a tight hole you have to trust your ability and feel as though you can hit a spanker. Sometimes it helps to cure a negative attitude by standing up there and throwing caution to the wind. Let it rip – at least that way you know your swing is free and you release smoothly through the ball.

Think your way around

The width of the fairway needn't be small for the landing area to be tight. Fairway bunkers are sometimes positioned in awkward places around driving distance. Strategy is all important. So when you find a hole with cunning traps that you know you can reach, think carefully.

A driver may leave you a shorter shot than hitting an iron from the tee, but it also flirts with the danger. It takes an exacting strike to thread your ball through the gap. You gain very little by going for the driver – even if you hit a good one – as your approach is tricky. You have to fly a trap and land the ball softly to hold the shallow green.

Hitting an iron or fairway wood short of the trap is much safer and leaves you a better approach. Though your second is longer than from a driver, you have a clear line into the flag and more green to work with.

masterclass

On line Ollie

José-Maria Olazabal blitzed his way to one of the most sensational victories of recent times in the 1990 World Series. Only four players broke par for the week on the 7149yd (6537m) Firestone Country Club course. But, remarkably, the Spaniard was 18 under – 12 strokes ahead of nearest rival Lanny Wadkins.

His record opening 61 followed by three 67s was a superb exhibition of long, straight, controlled hitting on one of the toughest and tightest courses on the US Tour.

José conquered the narrow fairways flanked by thick rough using a combination of sound, powerful technique and clever strategy. He realized that hitting the fairways was more important than length, so opted to play a 1 iron from the tee on many occasions.

Though it often left him a long distance away – perhaps even a wood – he had more chance of making his par or birdie than from 20yd (18m) further up but just off the fairway.

Sidehill Lies

While developing your golf swing you tend to practice from a flat lie. It won't be long, however, before your ball lands on a hill and you have to adjust your shot. On a sidehill lie your feet are on the same level, but the ball is higher or lower.

You need to practice hitting from these lies to find out just what effect different slopes have on the shape of the shot as it flies through the air. Often with a sidehill lie your ball curves quite dramatically to the right or the left.

Once familiar with the shot from a sidehill lie you'll be able to judge just how far left or right you must aim to compensate for this curve.

BALL ABOVE YOUR FEET

Before setting up the shot you need to choose the correct club for the distance. For better control, grip down the club. This also compensates for the ball lying higher than your feet.

The higher a ball is above your feet the further left it flies. Once

PLAYING THE SHOT
Hitting from a sidehill lie is difficult – only a small part of the sole of the clubhead touches the ground at impact. You must adjust your posture and change your aim to achieve a balanced set-up. You may also need to shorten your swing for a sharper strike.

BALL BELOW LEVEL OF FEET

1 SET-UP
To compensate for the left-to-right flight of the ball, aim the clubface and align your body left of the target. Let your weight rest on your heels for a firm balance.

2 BACKSWING
As your back is more bent you take the club away sharply, which leads to a steep swing plane. Make a three-quarter backswing. At the top the club points left of target.

3 STAY DOWN
Keep your head down through impact for as long as possible. If you don't you fall off the stroke, topping the ball or sending it flying to the right.

STOOP TO CONQUER

The further below your feet the ball is, the more bent your back becomes and the steeper the swing plane is. At address your hands are lower than normal and most of your weight is on your heels. It is one of the hardest shots in golf.

NORMAL SET-UP

BALL BELOW FEET

4 REDUCED BODY TURN
The followthrough is more restricted than usual because your bent posture limits body rotation. Your weight finishes on your left side.

BALL ABOVE LEVEL OF FEET

① ADDRESSING THE BALL
Aim and align right of target to compensate for the right-to-left flight. Grip down the club. Your posture is more upright than on level ground.

② BACKSWING
Make as full a swing as you can control – a three-quarter one is comfortable. Keep your balance for a crisp strike. At the top the club points right of target.

③ SMOOTH TEMPO
Keep a smooth tempo on the downswing. Your swing is slightly flatter than normal with the clubhead traveling across your body from out to in at impact.

STAND UP TO THE BALL

④ BALANCED FOLLOWTHROUGH
The followthrough should be the same length as the backswing. Your hands finish lower than usual because the flatter swing plane pulls them around your body.

The higher above your feet the ball is, the more upright your back and the flatter your swing plane becomes. Your hands are also higher than normal. It's easier to strike a ball above your feet than below them.

FEET BELOW BALL

NORMAL SET-UP

you have chosen a club, visualize how far left your shot will go and draw an imaginary line right of the target to compensate.

Aim the clubhead along this line and align your body parallel to it. Take special care to check that you are not automatically aligning your body parallel to the ball-to-target line.

THE SWING

Your posture is affected by the slope. With the ball above your feet your back is more upright than normal which causes a flatter swing plane.

Make as full a swing as you can control, and concentrate on timing the strike correctly – your set-up changes should take care of the rest. Confidence is essential for a successful swing. Assume that the ball will come back straight even though you are aiming to the right.

When you play the shot correctly, the ball begins its flight to the right and slowly curves around to your target. The ball will draw (spin in a counterclockwise direction) so allow for it to roll after landing.

BALL BELOW YOUR FEET

Many golfers find it difficult to hit a ball lying below their feet – they tend to lose their balance or swing on top of the ball. Perfect your

Adjust your aim

BALL FLIES RIGHT

BALL FLIES LEFT

BALL BELOW FEET

FEET BELOW BALL

The ball doesn't fly straight from a sidehill lie because the slope influences the path of the clubhead. The steeper the slope the further off line your ball travels.

When the ball is below your feet the clubhead is pulled across the slope from right to left (out-to-in), causing a slight fade. The ball curves to the right. Aim the clubface and align your body left of the target to compensate.

When the ball is higher than your feet, the clubhead sweeps along the slope from left to right (in-to-out) producing a slight draw. The ball curves to the left. To compensate aim the clubface and align your body right of the target.

Note how only a small part of the clubhead sole touches the ground at impact – near the heel (ball below feet) and near the toe (feet below ball).

address position to help you make a balanced swing.

Because the ball is low you stoop over it, causing a more upright swing plane. The ball curves from left to right. You may lose distance with this shot, so for a balanced, easy swing it's essential that you use a less lofted club.

ADDRESSING THE BALL

Decide how much the ball will move from left to right and set the club accordingly. Align your body parallel to your chosen line. Adopt your normal posture but place slightly more weight back on your heels. This stops you losing your balance as you swing. Your knees are more flexed than usual.

You have to bend over more – how much depends on the steepness of the slope – and grip down the club slightly if you need more control. If you feel unstable place more weight back on your heels or increase the width of your stance.

SLOW TEMPO

Concentrate on keeping a slow tempo and swing the club only three-quarters of the way back and through. Remember you are using a less lofted club so distance shouldn't be a problem if you make a clean strike.

As with all awkward shots, assume a confident attitude and stay with the shot – don't pull away on your downswing. If you do, you will certainly top the ball from this type of sidehill lie.

pro tip

Grip down for sharp strike

If the ball is on a different level from your feet grip down the shaft for greater control. Because just a tiny area of the sole of the clubface touches the ground at impact, there is only a small margin for error.

To increase your chances of a solid strike slide your hands about 2in (5cm) further down the shaft than normal. The closer your hands are to the ball the more control and better clubhead feel you have.

Ball Perched up in Rough

The perched lie is one of the most misunderstood shots in golf because you don't come across it often. It can be just as demanding as dislodging your ball from a half buried lie in rough.

Ignore your usual rules concerning rough play. It's essential you sweep the ball away like a wood shot from a tee peg. Don't strike down into impact, as you do with a normal shot from long grass.

One of the most reliable methods for clipping the ball sweetly off a perched lie is to grip down the club slightly and make a three-quarter swing. Try to quiet down the movement of your wrists on the backswing. Also position the ball a fraction further forward in your stance than you would normally.

SITTING PRETTY
At first glance your ball may look as though it's resting invitingly on a tee peg, but a perched lie in the rough is no time to be complacent. It's one of those rare occasions in golf where the lie looks better than it actually is. You must sweep the ball away for best results. Don't strike down steeply like a normal rough recovery shot.

SUCCEED FROM A PERCHED LIE

② SHALLOW START
You must create a shallow swing arc from the start because this is the key to sweeping the ball away on the downswing. Concentrate on drawing the club back wide and low to the ground. Reducing the amount of wrist break helps you achieve this, and at the same time ensures the club doesn't travel too steeply on the backswing. Stop the club just short of horizontal to increase your clubhead control – vital from an unusual lie.

① NEW ADDRESS
There are two changes you can make to your address when the ball rests on a perched lie – either hover the clubhead or choke down on the grip. Each helps you strike correctly, so choose the one you feel most comfortable with. Also, position the ball a little further forward than you normally would to encourage the sweeping action through impact.

Rough rider
Aiming straight at the target is unwise if the ball is perched a long way above the level of your feet. It's the same as playing from a sloping lie, so you're almost certain to drag the ball left of the flag.
  Align right of target – how far depends on the severity of the perched lie – and allow for the ball to draw back on line with the flag. Your swing plane becomes more rounded with the ball above your feet, so this change in flight path should happen naturally.

All of these factors help ensure that the clubhead reaches the bottom of its arc at the precise moment of impact, thus giving you the shallow angle of attack that you need. Less grass is taken in comparison to a normal shot from rough, and the clubhead sweeps the ball away.

STROKE WITH DISTANCE

One very positive aspect of the perched lie is that it doesn't prevent you from gaining as much height and distance as you require. You're not restricted in your club selection.
  Because of the shallow angle at

which the clubhead meets the ball, this shot doesn't generate a great deal of backspin. So don't expect the ball to stop quickly, unless you're firing into a sponge-like green in the distance.
  The ball travels at least one club further, possibly two, from a perched lie, so choke down on the grip to compensate. This small adjustment in technique reduces the width of your swing arc. Taking this into account you can probably hit the same club as you would from a normal lie.
  Make sure you allow for a little more run on the ball. Backspin is hard to generate because you're not hitting down on the ball. So if

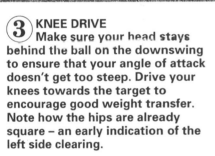

③ KNEE DRIVE
Make sure your head stays behind the ball on the downswing to ensure that your angle of attack doesn't get too steep. Drive your knees towards the target to encourage good weight transfer. Note how the hips are already square – an early indication of the left side clearing.

④ SWEPT AWAY
A combination of good moves help you sweep the ball away. By the nature of the strike less grass is taken at impact – this is a positive sign because it means you haven't chopped down too steeply on the ball. Note the impressive firm left side, providing solid resistance against which you can release the clubhead through square towards the target.

the ground is hard, or there's a strong wind at your back, your ball can easily run out of control on landing.

If you create an angle of attack that is just too steep, the clubhead can easily cut underneath the ball. A miss-hit from the top part of the blade is likely to happen depressingly often. This results in a shot that flies very little distance through the air.

PERCHED PITCHING

The rules for playing a short shot from a perched lie are the same as from long range. The ball sits up nicely for you, so the critical move

is sweeping it away cleanly rather than striking down.

Grip down the club and hover the blade at the same level to the ball. This simple, and very important, change in address promotes a clean strike.

WRIST REMINDER

Also reduce the amount of wrist break on the backswing because this is the most effective way to promote a shallow angle of attack on the downswing.

If you have any doubts about the use of your wrists, remember one very constructive rule of thumb – the more you hinge your

wrists on the way back, the steeper the arc at which the clubhead approaches the ball. On the other hand, no wrist break produces a very shallow angle of attack – more of a sweeping action in fact.

WISE CHOICE

Allow for more run on the ball when you chip off a perched lie. You're likely to find a mid iron more reliable than your sand wedge from the same position.

Provided you target a flat landing area – preferably on the putting surface – it's easier to predict the progress of your ball on the ground than it is through the air.

pro tip

✔ CLEAN LIE

CLUBHEAD TRAVELS
ON DOWNWARD
PATH – CRISP STRIKE

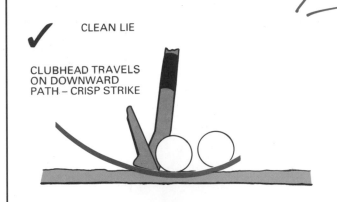

✗ PERCHED LIE

ANGLE OF ATTACK TOO
STEEP – BALL STRUCK
WITH TOP OF CLUBHEAD

Angled approach

Success from a perched lie hinges completely on the angle at which the clubhead approaches the ball. Whichever club you have in your hands, the swing arc around impact must be shallow. Your aim should be to sweep the ball away, much in the way you do with a driver off the tee.

Poor strikes stem from the misguided belief that because you're in the rough you have to strike down on the ball. If you create a steep arc, you run the risk of striking the ball with the top part of the clubhead. Misunderstanding the fundamentals causes your downfall – not any lack of ability.

✔

SHALLOW ANGLE
OF ATTACK

CLUBHEAD SWEEPS
BALL AWAY

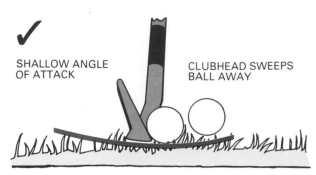

On the bright side

A perched lie usually means you have to work extra hard at producing the right result. However, if you need to play a lob shot over a bunker, having your ball sitting up is a definite advantage.

Concentrate on your set-up. Align your shoulders, hips and feet left of target. Aim the clubface straight at the flag and make a full swing, keeping your wrists out of the swing as much as possible.

There's a certain security about this shot, because it's almost impossible for your ball to fly wildly out of control. If you play it correctly, the ball flies high and lands softly.

Unpredictable Lies

An unpredictable lie around the green is a cruel slice of luck. The ball may be lying down or sitting up, on unforgiving bare ground or in a divot.

If you're extremely unlucky you may be faced with a combination of more than one problem, with an awkward stance or perhaps a bunker in front of you to add to your troubles.

But unpredictable lies happen to every golfer – from the experienced professional to the raw beginner – and on all types of course. While no one can expect to get up and down in 2 shots every time, it's important you learn how to handle each situation so you can limit the damage to your score.

LIE DETECTOR

The lie of your ball is the main reason the shot is made difficult, so think about this first. Depending on how you see the shot, the lie determines the club you use.

From a bare lie on hard ground a pitching wedge is the ideal club – particularly if you need a little height on the shot. The leading edge is fairly straight and most suited to nipping the ball cleanly from unforgiving surfaces. If there are no hazards to carry, a less lofted iron is an effective and safe club to use.

A thin sends the ball shooting across the green and is the most common fault off hard ground. Avoid using the sand wedge – it has a wide, rounded flange and the clubhead easily bounces into the middle of the ball at impact. A sand wedge is also unsuitable from a bare lie on soft ground. The rounded sole of the clubhead

SHORT GAME SHARPNESS
Each shot from an unpredictable lie is demanding in its own way – you need to judge which club is best suited for the job and predict how the ball behaves. Basic techniques help you escape from most situations, but occasionally you have to be inventive in your approach. By combining the fundamentals of the short game with a lively imagination, no situation should hold any fear.

CLOSE TO THE EDGE

1 OPEN STANCE
Loose sand around the edge of bunkers presents you with a testing lie, but it's more predictable than it looks. Align your feet, hips and shoulders left of target and aim the clubface at the flag. Feel free to ground the club behind the ball.

2 PICK UP
Swing the club back steeply outside the line. Let your wrists hinge so that the shaft of the club and your left arm form a right angle. The club points almost straight up – don't allow it to travel any further or you risk losing control.

3 SPLASH DOWN
Concentrate on splashing the clubhead down on a mark about 1in (2.5cm) behind the ball. Generate lots of clubhead speed into impact – the ball is unlikely to travel too far, but if you do miss the green it's better to be long than in the bunker.

4 HIGH FLOATER
Stay down long after the ball pops up in the air for its soft landing on the green. The back of the left hand stays ahead of the clubhead to prevent the face closing – never let your right hand roll over the left through impact.

digs in behind the ball – the result is a frustrating duffed chip.

From clinging rough the emphasis is on striking down steeply into impact. From short range use a sand wedge. Keep your hands forward at address with the ball central in your stance. Break your wrists quickly on the backswing and strike down crisply into the bottom of the ball.

Loose sand outside the bunker under your ball can act as a cushion at impact if you play the shot correctly. Treat it as you would a normal bunker shot and hit down with a sand wedge into the sand behind the ball. Accelerate on the downswing and you can be confident of a satisfactory result – the ball floats high on to the green and lands softly.

Unless the sand is very compact don't try to strike the ball cleanly. Your margin for error is tiny and even the slightest miss-hit results in disaster. The chances are you play your next shot from sand, too, but from the bunker in front of you this time.

TAKING A STANCE

When you have an awkward stance as well as an unpredictable lie, sound technique helps you cope with every shot. Remember, the ball reacts according to the slope of the ground.

On an uphill lie the ball flies higher than normal – downhill the reverse is true – so make allowances when you judge the roll of the ball on landing. With the ball below your feet the shot flies to the right – when it's above your feet the ball drifts to the left.

The basic chipping stroke stands you in good stead in unpredictable lies, but you may also

Once is enough
Finding your ball lying in a divot mark is very frustrating and the result of someone else's thoughtlessness. One such experience alone should encourage you to replace your own divots every time. If replaced immediately the turf makes a quick and full recovery – it's also one less divot mark on the course for your ball to land in.

Predict the unpredictable
Divot marks wouldn't be on a golf course in a perfect world, but alas this isn't the case. There is very little margin for error from this lie – the clubhead may dig into the ground causing a duff. A thinned shot also happens all too easily if your technique is incorrect. You must keep your hands ahead of the ball and strike down steeply into the bottom of the ball.

Hard ground tests your technique in the hot summer months when the fairways become parched. The danger is of the clubhead bouncing off the hard, unforgiving surface into the middle of the ball – a thinned shot is the depressing result. Avoid using the sand wedge from a bare lie – the wide flange bounces more than any other club. Use a straighter faced iron and nip the ball cleanly off the surface.

High on a tuft of grass your ball is precariously placed – the outcome can be disastrous if you don't play the shot correctly. Your normal swing with an iron sends the clubhead on a downward path into impact, but you must guard against chopping clean underneath the ball and causing a dreaded air shot. Grip further down the club than normal and hover the clubhead above the ground at address to promote a clean strike. It's important to accelerate into the ball – don't quit on the shot or you risk a double hit.

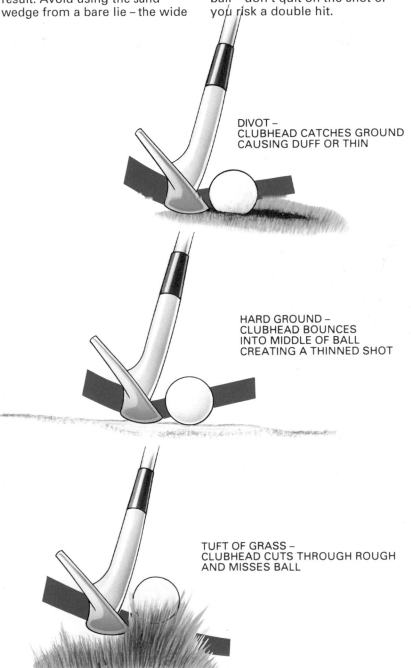

DIVOT –
CLUBHEAD CATCHES GROUND
CAUSING DUFF OR THIN

HARD GROUND –
CLUBHEAD BOUNCES
INTO MIDDLE OF BALL
CREATING A THINNED SHOT

TUFT OF GRASS –
CLUBHEAD CUTS THROUGH ROUGH
AND MISSES BALL

BALL PERCHED IN THE AIR

①STURDY STANCE
While it doesn't happen too often, the sight of a ball perched high up on a tuft of grass fills many golfers with dread. But for a shot of 80yd (73m) you can hit the green every time. Your stance is awkward, so make sure you're balanced at address.

②TAKING BACK
Your main thought is to strike the ball cleanly, so grip down the club. Hover the clubhead above the ground to help you take the club smoothly away from the ball. Make a normal backswing and break your wrists halfway back.

⑤OUT ON RELEASE
Most of your weight is now on the left side to put you in a strong position in the hitting area. Let your hands release through impact and stay down on the shot until you feel your arms pull your body up naturally.

⑥BALL FLIES HIGH
As always, a good controlled swing results in a perfectly balanced followthrough – there's no toppling back from this position. The clubhead throws the ball – and plenty of grass – high into the air.

③ TOP OF BACKSWING
Concentrate on turning your shoulders fully and stop short of horizontal to stay in control of the club. Keep your legs flexed and head very still to prevent your body coming up off the ball.

④ LEFT IN CHARGE
Focus your eyes on the back of the ball and pull the club down with your left hand dominating the swing. Drive your right knee towards the target to help you transfer your weight on to the left side.

need to improvise a little to play a shot precisely.

Treat every situation as a challenge and take time to compose yourself. Be creative and use your imagination – there's an effective way to play a shot from every lie. All good shots are enjoyable – but a successful escape from an unpredictable lie is extremely satisfying and a tremendous boost to your confidence.

There are no short cuts to mastering escapes from difficult situations, so don't expect a shot to come off first time. Every golfer knows the difficulties of those awkward shots near the green. If you don't know what to do, you're in for a frustrating time as you helplessly watch good scores deteriorate through sloppy short shots.

Try to find time in your practice sessions to experiment with shots from different lies – you learn to remove some of the element of chance and judge how the ball reacts. You can then create the shot in your mind and be confident of playing it correctly.

pro tip

Deep in trouble
If your ball comes to rest in a deep divot mark, or one that points way off line, you're faced with a serious problem. It's hard to judge how the ball reacts, so look to play the shot with the greatest margin for error.

Playing along the line of the divot is usually the best option. You must strike down sharply into the bottom of the ball – expect a very low flight on the shot and plenty of run.

DIVOT SHOT

1 MAKING A STANCE
A ball in a divot mark is one of the most daunting lies you find on a golf course. Providing the divot points at the target and isn't too deep, the shot is not nearly as fearsome as it looks. Stand open to the ball-to-target line with the clubface aiming at the flag.

2 SHORT AND STEEP
Pick the club up steeply by hinging your wrists as you swing your arms back. Keep your body very still and your weight towards the left side – if you sway away from the ball you're likely to thin the shot through the green or move the ball no distance at all.

3 BALL TO TURF CONTACT
Accelerate the club down into the bottom of the ball making sure you keep your tempo smooth. It's very much a hands and arms shot, so avoid body movement. The clubhead strikes the ball first and then the ground.

4 FIRM WRISTS
Keep your left wrist firm and ahead of the clubhead through impact. The ball often flies lower than from a normal lie and may overshoot the target, but that's better than a heavy duff which moves the ball no distance at all.

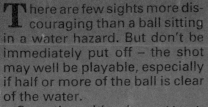

Playing out of Water

There are few sights more discouraging than a ball sitting in a water hazard. But don't be immediately put off – the shot may well be playable, especially if half or more of the ball is clear of the water.

Sometimes it's wise *not* to attempt the shot. This forces a 1-stroke penalty which allows you to drop the ball back on dry ground.

Know your capabilities and practice playing from different water hazards so you learn to judge when to play the shot and when to take a penalty. While the high handicapper may panic and be best off dropping the ball, the advanced golfer can often save strokes by playing the shot.

ANALYZE THE SITUATION

Weigh up the advantages and disadvantages of hitting a par-

THINK POSITIVELY
For the advanced player, hitting out of water is often a better option than taking a penalty. If the ball lands in shallow water and you feel capable of clearing the bank, play the shot – you may save yourself a valuable stroke.

THE WATER SHOT

①CAREFUL PREPARATION
Take a firm footing, as if in a bunker. Keep the clubhead just above the water, taking care not to let the club touch anything inside the hazard. If the lie of the ball is good, aim for the green.

②STEEP ANGLE OF ATTACK
Take the club back with your arms and hands. An early wrist break helps produce the necessary lift to get the ball over the bank. Don't lose confidence – it's important to keep an even rhythm throughout.

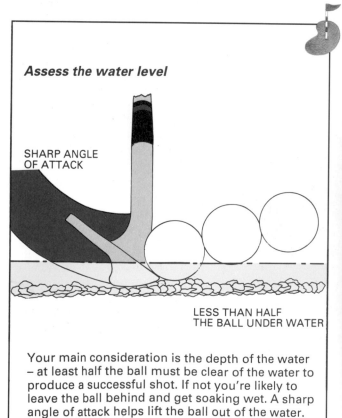

Assess the water level

SHARP ANGLE
OF ATTACK

LESS THAN HALF
THE BALL UNDER WATER

Your main consideration is the depth of the water – at least half the ball must be clear of the water to produce a successful shot. If not you're likely to leave the ball behind and get soaking wet. A sharp angle of attack helps lift the ball out of the water.

ticular shot from water. If the green is not in range it's best to accept a penalty and drop the ball. But if you are near the green or you can appreciably shorten the distance along the fairway, you may well be saving the vital shot in a close game.

When playing the ball from a ditch or stream you probably have to clear a bank. If you feel that the shot is too difficult even with your most lofted club, it is best not to play it – your lack of confidence could well lead to disaster. Play safe. Take the penalty instead.

The ball must be at least half clear of the water and sitting on a firm surface for you to lift it out. The club may sink into a soft surface, making the shot extremely risky.

It is very difficult to assess the exact striking point when part of the ball is beneath the water. The effect of light through water makes the ball appear bigger and further away.

PREPARATION FOR THE SHOT

Once you decide to play the shot your next consideration is keeping yourself dry. A water shot is rather like an explosion shot from a bunker – a great deal of water splashes as you strike the ball. For complete protection wear water-proof gear.

Another sensible measure when the ball lands in deep water is to remove your shoes and socks. Have a towel ready for when you come out of the water and remember to dry the club as well.

PLAY WITH CONFIDENCE

Generally for water shots the best club to use is the sand wedge. Because of its high angle of loft it really lifts the ball, especially over a bank. The sand wedge is also the heaviest club so it travels through the water smoothly.

Before you enter the water visualize the precise path that the ball will take towards your chosen target. This helps you to develop confidence in the shot, preventing the most common cause of disaster – anxiety.

The rules concerning water shots are very similar to the ones for bunker play. You incur a 2-stroke penalty if your club makes

3 MAKING CONTACT
You usually need to strike the water just before the ball. How far behind the ball you strike depends on how much of it is submerged, but ½in (1.5cm) is a good guide to follow.

4 SMOOTH THROUGHSWING
It is vital to maintain a smooth, even tempo as you follow through – the water slows down the path of the club considerably. Don't hesitate with the shot – even if water is flying in your face.

contact with anything inside the hazard before your downswing. This rule applies even in summer when the hazards may be dry.

Take a couple of practice swings above the water to get the feel of your shot. If about half of the ball is submerged in the water, you need to focus on a point about ½in (1.5cm) behind the ball.

The ball should be on the inside of your left heel – near the green use a slightly open stance. If you need to lift the ball sharply out of the hazard, open the clubface and aim an appropriate amount to the left to compensate.

An early break of the wrists on the backswing also helps to produce a steep angle of attack.

Above all, make sure that you maintain confidence in the shot and keep your eyes on the clubhead as it strikes the ball.

Beware the stiff penalty

When playing from water your club must not touch anything within the confines of the hazard *before* your downswing begins. If it does, you are penalized 2 strokes.

The area is marked by colored posts or lines – don't forget that in most cases the grass on the bank is also part of the hazard.

To avoid the penalty don't ground the club at address. Make sure that you create a steep angle of attack as this limits the risk of contact with the hazard.

masterclass

Marsh in the wet

Australian Graham Marsh came across trouble at the 8th hole in the 1985 Lawrence Batley International at The Belfry. He hit his second shot on this par-4 hole into a water hazard near the green.

He recovered successfully by chipping the ball out onto the green and finished off with a 12ft (3.7m) putt. His confidence in tackling the shot under pressure saved his par – he went on to win the competition.

Awkward Stances

Escaping from trouble on a golf course doesn't just mean playing the run of the mill shots – such as a straightforward splash shot from sand. You're often faced with a shot that needs imagination and an improvised swing.

When your ball finds a tricky spot, be ready and willing to adapt both your body position and technique for a safe and sometimes attacking getaway.

BALANCING ACT

The key to playing from an awkward lie when your stance is hampered is to stay balanced throughout the stroke. Concentrate on your posture, and then try to swing as normally as possible.

Experiment with your stance before you play. Shift and fiddle around until you feel comfortable and stable. However, you must realize that finding the most secure posture doesn't necessarily mean you can play the most productive shot.

Try to find a stance that gives you the freedom of movement to play a meaningful recovery – even if it means you have to stand in a slightly unfamiliar and compromising way.

SEE THE SHOT

Take time to choose your club and go through the stroke in your mind several times before you play. Decide which shape of swing you want. Then practice the backswing and the start of your downswing to see if either are impeded and if your balance holds true.

Also check the throughswing path to find out whether you need

to modify it – perhaps having to stop it short so that the club doesn't crash into a tree.

Always swing smoothly – a jerky, forced action often fails to free the ball – and stay as steady as possible throughout the stroke.

Too much movement during the

swing makes it hard to return the blade precisely to the ball.

Never try to overhit the shot – be content to knock the ball back onto the fairway if firing for the green is likely to go wrong. This cautious approach should save you shots in the long run.

STRADDLE-LEGGED
Often it's not possible to adopt a normal stance to play a shot. Imagination and a clever modification of your set-up mean you can turn a near disaster into a positive result. With the ball well below your feet, standing wide-legged astride the ball helps you to reach it, and if you stay balanced and steady you can play a powerful and accurate stroke.

BACK TO BARK

1 UPRIGHT STANCE

To cope with a ball that's landed close to an obstruction, it may still be possible to squeeze between ball and obstacle and play a positive shot. Adapt your stance and swing so that you can still move the club freely without hitting the tree.

2 HIGH BACKLIFT

Standing upright means you have to pick up the club sharply to avoid the tree. It's better to swing it up almost over your head than try for a near normal action if it means you lessen the risk of hitting the obstruction. This shot is nearly all hands and arms, so you must swing smoothly with control if you're to strike the ball properly.

3 EASY TEMPO

Since your action is unfamiliar, concentrate on swinging down with an easy tempo and rhythm so that the clubhead meets the ball squarely. Look at the back of the ball – this improves your eye, hand coordination and increases the chance of the shot coming off. Don't dip down into impact – stay upright – otherwise you can easily stab behind the ball.

4 CONTROLLED FINISH

Swing through keeping the blade going straight at the target so that the club doesn't crash into the tree. Stop the throughswing shorter than normal to help avoid a collision. If you're firm and controlled through the ball there is no reason why your shot can't fly powerfully straight.

HEAD START

1 BEND AT THE WAIST
Finding a balanced and stable stance is crucial to the success of any awkward shot. To cope with a ball on a steep downward slope, adopt a straddle-legged position – where your feet are set at well over shoulder width apart. Bend over from the waist more than usual to help you reach the ball. Once you have found a comfortable stance, feel how your body is positioned, as it's vital to keep it the same throughout the swing to be sure of making good contact with the ball.

2 NO LIFTING
Make your backswing while keeping the head perfectly still. Note that its position at the top of the backswing is the same as at address. Resist the temptation to rise up into your usual body position – this is bound to lead to a miss-hit, as you must dip back down to have a chance of connecting at all with the ball. Even though your swing is hampered and likely to be more arms than lower body, strive for a full shoulder turn, but not at the expense of overbalancing.

3 LEVEL ATTACK
Swing smoothly down into impact. Don't force the shot – this helps you stay balanced and gives you a greater chance of hitting a crisp stroke. Notice how the head has stayed in the same position throughout the back and downswing. Though you can't swing as powerfully or fluently as normal, it's still possible to attack the ball with vigor.

4 POISE AT THE FINISH
The only time you should rise up and into a more normal swing position is after impact. Trying to stay in the bent posture throughout the swing means you can't release the club properly. You probably overbalance and fall forward – in this case with dire consequences. Moving through into this upright finish also helps you to hit the ball powerfully.

Up a tree

When you're in difficulties close to an obstacle, it's vital to practice your swing several times to find a clear path. Once you have found a route along which you can swing freely, make sure your action is controlled.

If you try to force the shot you swing on a slightly different path than you intended, and the results are disastrous. There is a good chance of your club tangling with the obstacle on either the back or downswing.

The worst possible scene is when you start down towards impact and you clip a tree. This throws your rhythm and balance well out and it's easy to hit an air shot.

Temper your desire to hit a forceful shot with a sense of safety – never take on too much.

Mac's predicament

It isn't just amateurs who find themselves in a jam now and then – top pros land in trouble too.

In the final of the 1990 World Matchplay Championship at Wentworth, Mark McNulty put himself in a tricky spot on the 12th. His second to the par 5 finished dangerously close to the out of bounds fence. He had to improvise.

Mac backed up against the fence which meant that the ball was much closer to his toes than normal. The problem was that if he swung back and through with a square blade along the line of the fence to avoid clipping it, the ball would not fly at the target. A slight closing of the blade and he was looking at a big score – as the ball could easily fly over the fence.

To play an accurate shot Mark

made his downswing while holding the back of his left hand – and hence his blade – open in relation to his feet but square to the target. The ball came out well but landed just short of the green.

Unfortunately for Mac, Ian Woosnam took 2 putts and made his birdie. Even though the Zimbabwean had made a good recovery it couldn't prevent Woosie walking off with the title.

Maximize your Ability

Many professionals could have been born with a golf club in their hands. Seve Ballesteros is one such golfer – while he has worked extremely hard at his game from an early age, Ballesteros is blessed with wonderful natural ability.

Unfortunately, the rest of the golfing population aren't quite so lucky. For the mere mortal, even hard work cannot guarantee the reward of playing off scratch one day.

Even so, Ben Hogan believes that all average golfers are capable of breaking 80 regularly, provided they go about their golf intelligently and constructively.

If you want to be as good as you possibly can, learn how to make the most of the talents at your disposal – this is the key to avoiding years of frustration and endless near misses.

Many club golfers strike the ball well enough to play off single figures, yet have handicaps in the high teens – a terrible waste. Probably the biggest culprit is a sloppy short game.

Don't tolerate serious errors on your chipping and putting – you cannot make the most of your ability if your short game doesn't allow it. A failure to convert good striking into good scores can also become very tiresome.

You may fail to make the most of your ability for different reasons. Maybe you lack something when it comes to course management – the game is there but you make poor shotmaking decisions. Or perhaps you spray the ball

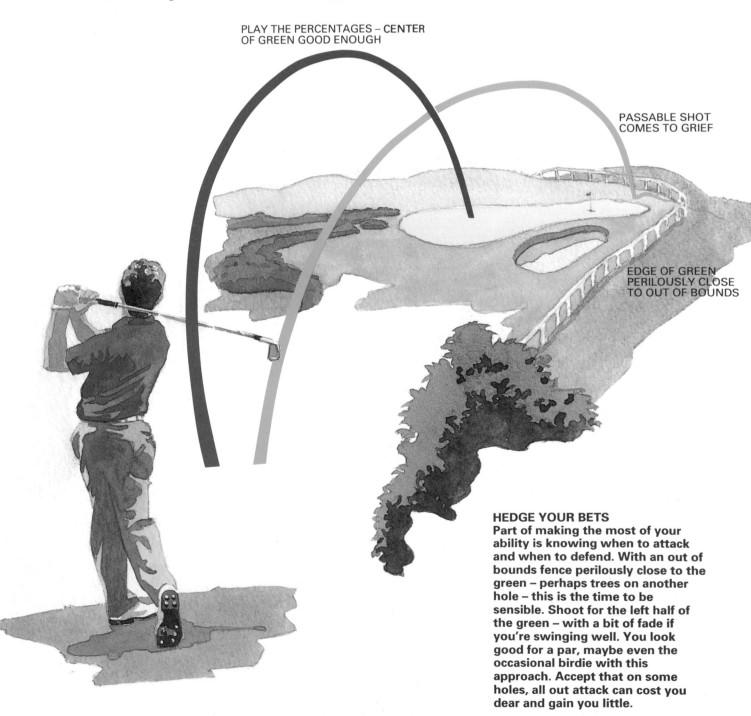

PLAY THE PERCENTAGES – CENTER OF GREEN GOOD ENOUGH

PASSABLE SHOT COMES TO GRIEF

EDGE OF GREEN PERILOUSLY CLOSE TO OUT OF BOUNDS

HEDGE YOUR BETS
Part of making the most of your ability is knowing when to attack and when to defend. With an out of bounds fence perilously close to the green – perhaps trees on another hole – this is the time to be sensible. Shoot for the left half of the green – with a bit of fade if you're swinging well. You look good for a par, maybe even the occasional birdie with this approach. Accept that on some holes, all out attack can cost you dear and gain you little.

THE REWARDS FOR GREAT PUTTING

NORTH STAR
Many golfers have struck the ball better than Andy North, but few can boast two US Open titles to their name. North is the classic example of a golfer who has made the best of his ability by developing a highly unorthodox, yet remarkably effective putting stroke.

There are many lessons you can learn from North's career. One is not to be intimidated by impressive ball striking – this alone does not make someone a winner. Another is to appreciate the importance of developing a putting stroke you can rely on. You may never putt as well as Andy North, but you can probably tighten up your putting to the extent that it is sharper and more reliable than your current stroke.

pro tip

Your Achilles' heel
Every golfer has at least one weakness. It may not be quite so obvious with the professionals, but there's usually one particular shot they don't feel entirely comfortable with.

You probably know your own Achilles' heel all too well. While it's vital you work on improving this, it's just as important you play to your strengths so that you can avoid hitting your least favorite shot too often. There's nothing wrong with this attitude. It may seem negative, but it's more about making the most of your ability.

about off the tee, or miss too many approaches to the green with your pitching wedge.

Whatever the reason for your lack of progress – and you should know what handicap you feel you can realistically play off – it's vital you identify it and then work at correcting it. Everyone has at least one weakness, so be honest – what's yours and what can you do about it?

The benefit of hindsight
In every golfing year you are bound to have your share of highs and lows. This is why it's a good idea to keep a record of your performance in all competitions. Sit down and analyze which parts of your game need improving most. If you want to lower your handicap it's vital you know which aspects need a boost.

If you don't keep some sort of record, an entire year of golf can easily become one big blur, with only an occasional shot staying fresh in your memory. This is a shame because you cannot improve on something you don't remember very well.

LOOK BACK ON YOUR YEAR – ANALYZE YOUR STRENGTHS AND WEAKNESSES

THE WHOLE TRUTH

The 1991 European Tour statistics show exactly where the top pros made their money that year. They also show how there is much more to success than superb ball striking.

▲ MR. ACCURACY

John Bland is Mr. Accuracy on the European Tour. Hitting 78% of greens and 83% of fairways, he comes out first and second in the respective categories. Now look at his putting. Bland finished nowhere in this department of the game – and Bland finished 56th in the Order of Merit. Not a bad year by most standards, but not a good one when you consider he hit more greens than any other player.

▲ FINE TOUCH FEHERTY

David Feherty's vital statistics are equally telling. Feherty finished nowhere in fairways split or greens hit. But he putted better than any other golfer, averaging a miserly 28.5 putts per round. This enabled him to finish 14th on the Order of Merit – earning more than three times as much money as John Bland – and also make his Ryder Cup debut at Kiawah Island. Who said there was no truth in the old adage, "Drive for show and putt for dough"?

▶ CONFOUND THOSE STATISTICS

Just when you thought statistics were starting to mean something, along comes Steven Richardson. The outstanding new face of the '90s failed to make it into the top ten of any category – these include sand saves, fairways hit, putts per round, driving distance and greens in regulation. And where did Steven Richardson finish on the Order of Merit? Second.

PERFECT TIME FOR PRACTICE

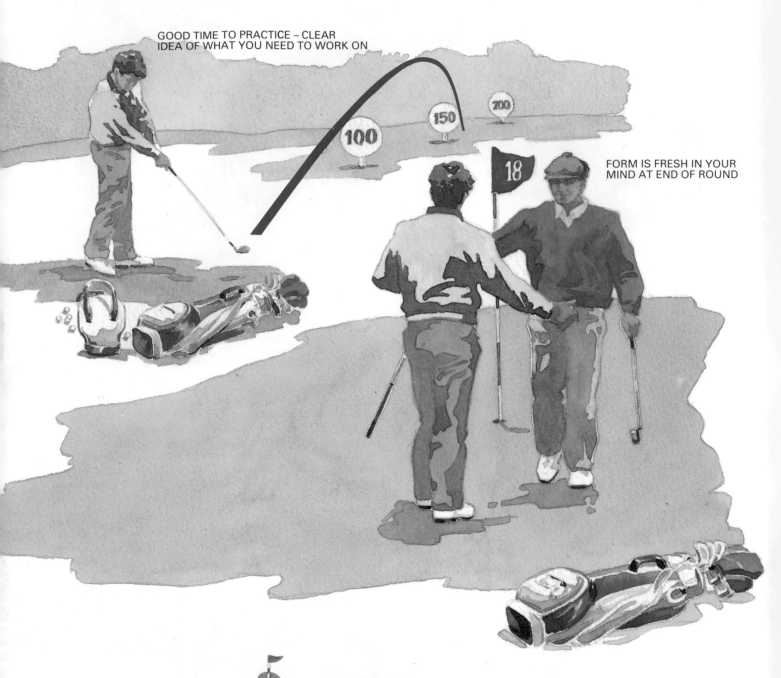

GOOD TIME TO PRACTICE – CLEAR
IDEA OF WHAT YOU NEED TO WORK ON

100   150   200

18

FORM IS FRESH IN YOUR
MIND AT END OF ROUND

Curtain raiser

Seeing Augusta National in full bloom makes most players feel the golfing year is about to begin. So for you, Masters week should be a good time to carry out some fine tuning on your equipment so that you're well prepared for the competitions at your club.

Having your clubs regripped is cheap and doesn't take long, but the effects are immediate and far more significant than many golfers believe. If you're a regular weekend player, you should have new grips on all of your clubs at least once a year.

FRESH IDEAS

Practice only benefits your game if you set about it in a constructive way – this means stepping onto the practice green with a clear objective in your mind of what you intend working on. Hit practice balls soon after you've finished a round, because you should remember which clubs you hit well and which you hit poorly. You can then set about correcting faults, improving strokes and grooving good moves into your game.

However, there are occasions when it's probably a bad idea to go and hit some practice balls – after a nightmare round is one instance. Here you've probably succeeded in achieving nothing but demoralizing yourself, so it's best to go home and think about something other than golf. This helps get the bad round out of your system before you hit another ball. Also, if the weather is absolutely foul, you're unlikely to benefit from a lonely hour on a bleak practice green.

Improving with Age

While few golfers would claim to be a better player at 50 than at 30, golf for seniors needn't be downhill all the way. Getting older means getting better – at least in some ways.

The secret to playing vintage golf is to work hard at upgrading certain departments of your game to compensate for others which deteriorate as the years slip by.

Loss of distance from the tee comes inevitably with age. Greens you used to hit comfortably in 2 are suddenly out of reach. And par 5s that used to yield you a stroke comfortably aren't quite the pushover they used to be.

This is why you have to be sharper with your wedge. You must occasionally roll in a raking putt and it's vital to be deadly from close range. Age is no barrier when it comes to the short game so make this your biggest strength.

ON THE BRIGHT SIDE

No golfer relishes the prospect of losing distance off the tee, especially if you've grown used to playing your second shot last in a group of four.

But hitting the ball shorter isn't all bad news. A loss of length often means an increase in accuracy. This is because most golfers' backswings become shorter with age, so there's generally less that

SMOOTH SWINGING SENIOR
Sam Snead shows that your golf game doesn't have to disintegrate as you grow older. The youngest man in history to shoot under his age – a 4 under par round of 66 when he was 67 – Snead's swing has changed over the years, but it's as smooth now as it ever was and works wonderfully well. You don't have to cling on to the swing you used as a youngster. It's natural to make minor alterations in technique to allow for the changes in your physique.

NEIL COLES – A LESSON FOR ALL SENIORS

AGELESS ABILITY
Golfers of a similar age to Neil Coles can learn a great deal simply by studying his swing. A regular winner in his European Tour days, former Ryder Cup stalwart and 1987 British Seniors Open Champion, Coles' technique has certainly stood the test of time. The message at address is one of comfort and relaxation.

FREEDOM OF MOVEMENT
For a man of his size – average height and build – Neil Coles has quite an upright stance. However, his arms hang down freely and his grip is light – each promotes an uninhibited swing of the club away from the ball. Note how the left shoulder turns under the chin from an early stage of the backswing.

PERFECT POSITION
Coles' position at the top of the backswing belies his age because the club easily reaches horizontal. Lifting his left heel off the ground helps him achieve this and can probably assist you in making a fuller upper body turn. However, swinging the club back to horizontal is not essential, so don't strain to emulate this aspect of Coles' swing.

TYPES OF SENIOR

WHICH ONE ARE YOU?	EXPERIENCED	BEGINNER
The senior golfer fits into one of two categories – the player who has just taken up the game, and the experienced golfer having to adapt to the physical aspects of the years rolling by. Whichever company of golfers you find yourself in, being a senior can have its advantages and disadvantages	The experienced senior golfer has a mental hurdle to overcome as you might not be capable of doing some of the things you used to do with ease. This can sometimes be hard to accept, but it's one of the key factors when it comes to success at all ages. Many senior golfers are wily old competitors, seldom doing much wrong and always hard to beat. This is all a matter of experience – there are no short cuts to improving this aspect of your game. Golf is one sport where older probably is wiser.	As a senior just taking up golf you have the advantage of improving all the time. However, it's vital to ingrain the basics right away. Early faults are always hard to iron out – this is even more true as you grow older. Taking up the game late in life generally means you need more professional training and advice on the right equipment.

POWER DRIVE
Coles stamps down his left heel to set the downswing in motion – this helps shift his weight towards the target and is a good tip if you have a tendency to fall backwards or find your weight stuck on the right side. Notice the tremendous drive of the legs and pull of the club with his left hand. This is where Coles starts to generate clubhead speed from a position known as the late hit.

PERFECT POSITION
Despite the hundreds of different types of swing, the position through impact is almost identical with all world class players. Notice how Coles' head remains behind the ball and how his left side clears, allowing him to drive the clubhead through to the target. Good technique and immaculate timing send the ball sailing into the distance.

GREAT FINISH
This is a wonderful followthrough position – it's perfectly balanced and places no strain on the lower back. Coles may not be the longest hitter in the world, but very few shots wander off line when you swing the club as well as he does.

pro tip

Generation gap
Make the most of golf club design and technology to find what's best for you. Equipment that works wonders for a 25-year-old may not be suited to a golfer of retirement age.
○ Try metal headed woods – they are more forgiving to miss-hits so fly straighter and consistently further.
○ Swap the steel shaft in your driver for a graphite or boron model. They're lighter and help generate clubhead speed.
○ If you have stiff shafts in all your clubs, change to regular. The extra flexibility in the shaft makes up for the possible lack of suppleness in your body.

can go wrong.

However, you need to make sure that the fundamentals such as set-up, alignment and grip are correct. If you're losing distance off the tee, you can't afford to stray off line very often.

The result of a good foundation and a compact swing should be to your liking. More of your drives should fly straight down the middle. You can enjoy playing more shots from the fairway, even if they're from a dozen paces further back than where you used to be.

HELP YOURSELF

If your shots aren't flying as far as they did ten years ago, play a two-piece surlyn-covered ball to give yourself maximum distance.

Many golfers fail to take this advice. Competing in a pro-am, Gary Player was once asked how he stopped the ball so quickly with his 3 iron from 200yd (183m). Player's immense ability and a balata ball helped contribute to this impressive result.

Player then asked the awe-struck amateur how far his ball traveled off a good 3 iron. The reply was 150yd (137m), to which Player said, "Why do you want to stop it quickly then?"

Learn from this – don't copy the pros if it doesn't help your game.

Advances in equipment enable you to do all you can to increase length, so make the most of them

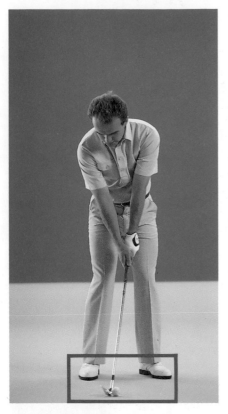

STROKE SAVER
If you're struggling to reach some par 4s in regulation, your final approach must be precise to stand a chance of making par. Therefore, the controlled pitch is a shot you should

practice regularly on the range. Remember the fundamentals:
○ Adopt a slightly open stance and position the ball centrally.
○ Keep your backswing compact. Three-quarter length is as far as you

should go. If you need to go further back, you need more club.
○ Make sure your hands are ahead of the ball at impact.
○ Think control throughout.

Tight restrictions
You're bound to feel less supple now than 20 years ago, so it's vital that you don't hinder movement any more than nature already has.

A tense grip doesn't just cause problems with your hand action – it restricts movement all over. Even good strikes don't travel far if your action is too stiff.

Make sure you grip the club lightly, but securely, with both hands – this promotes an uninhibited swish of the club through the ball.

HOME HELP
As you grow older, suppleness and flexibility are just as important as strength. You can develop these qualities at home by performing simple stretching exercises. Elastic straps are excellent for this. Available in most sports shops, this simple aid allows you to pull against some resistance.

whenever possible.

Bear in mind also that while you may envy the strength and energy of a younger player, you have the invaluable quality of experience to draw upon. You can't buy experience, and under pressure there's no substitute for it.

Experience also helps when it comes to course management and overall strategy. You should know and readily accept your limitations now. Youth tends to make golfers more likely to take risks.

Another positive aspect of growing older is that many people find they have more spare time on their hands. This is where you have an advantage over other golfers.

If you're fortunate enough to be in this position, and you have the desire to practice, make sure you devote more time to your chipping and putting than you do collectively to every other part of your game.

The short game is the one area of the course where physical attributes count for nothing, so you're on an even footing with your younger counterparts.

Master the Art of Scoring

MAKING IT WORK
There's an art to keeping a score together, particularly when things aren't going your way. One aspect of this is recovering from positions you might not set eyes on when you're playing well. The first lesson is not to become despondent – letting your head drop won't help you at all. See the situation as a challenge and use your imagination. Making a good escape from deep trouble is a very satisfying experience.

pro tip

The end result matters most
Some golfers feel embarrassed if they score well when their game is scrappy. Make sure you're not one of them. What would you rather have – first place playing badly or a lowly 20th striking the ball wonderfully?

Just because your game doesn't look pretty, it doesn't mean your scorecard should look ugly too. If you can play to your handicap hitting the ball badly, it's a compliment to your mental approach as well as your ability.

How many times have you hit the ball well and failed to play to your handicap? There's clearly something lacking in your game, although it can sometimes be hard to put your finger on the problem.

Equally there are days when everything you do seems to be a struggle. Even your favorite club in the bag can feel like something you've never laid hands on before.

This is where one of the main differences between good and bad players becomes clear. A good player accepts the fact that it's not going to be easy, knuckles down, then works hard at grinding out a respectable score.

Some inexperienced players give up when faced with difficulties. They become frustrated with a lack of form, often forgetting that the sole objective in golf is taking as few shots as possible. Their scores soon disintegrate.

BE SENSIBLE

Don't be too ambitious when you're off form. The cavalier approach is fine during a purple patch, but on an average day you need to be more canny.
○ Try and stick to a simple game plan and concentrate on the shots that are least likely to go wrong.

LIMIT THE DAMAGE

FIGHT YOUR WAY OUT OF TROUBLE
When your game isn't going well, no fairway looks wide enough for comfort. You grow sick of the sight of your ball careering into the woods. But stray tee shots needn't signal the beginning of the end. With care, you can escape with a lower score than you probably deserve from a bad drive.

On most par 4s – and particularly on par 5s where you can afford to take 3 to hit the green – one bad shot is seldom enough to run up a high score. Providing the trouble isn't too serious, there's usually easy access back on to the closely mown grass. This should prevent you from taking any more than 5 – certainly no disaster.

ONE GOOD ESCAPE GETS YOU OUT OF TROUBLE

POOR DRIVE LOOKS DISASTROUS FROM THE TEE

TACKLING DEEP TROUBLE

① LOW RUNNER
In this situation the rough presents the main problem. Overhanging branches add to the difficulty of the shot because you have to keep the ball low. A 7 or 8 iron is the ideal choice – a straighter faced club makes it hard to escape from the rough, whereas your sand wedge might pop the ball high into the air and hit the tree.

② SET THE ARC
Position the ball back in your stance and align slightly left of target. You need to create a steep arc on the backswing, so break your wrists slightly earlier than normal – this should enable you to hit down into the rough behind the ball.

③ ATTACKING DOWNSWING
The downswing for this shot is all about generating plenty of clubhead speed and really attacking the ball. Pull the club down hard with your left hand – you can't afford to be tentative because thick grass wraps around the clubhead through impact.

④ BE FIRM
In thick rough, you must be firm through the ball above all else. Keep your wrists rigid through impact – feel as though you almost punch the clubhead through the grass. The ball should shoot out fairly low and the clubhead take out a large clump of wiry grass.

PERCENTAGE PLAY

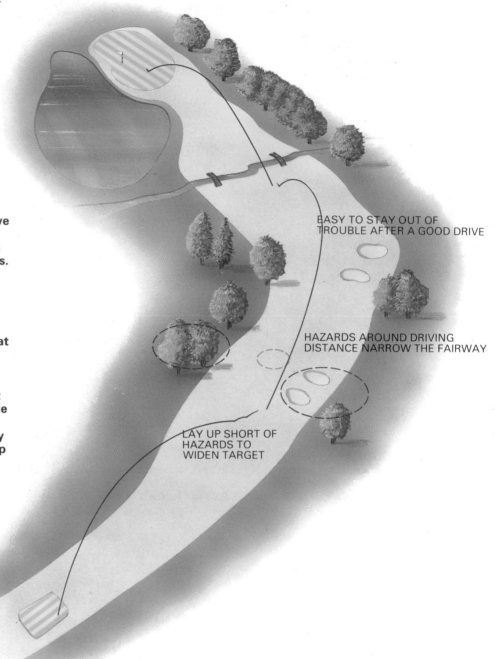

IDENTIFY TARGETS

If things aren't going well, widen your target area whenever you have the chance. On most holes trouble comes in stages – perhaps a clutch of bunkers or a small copse of trees. Hazards are seldom scattered the entire length of a fairway, so if you're off form, don't flirt with them.

On this par 5, bunkers and trees make the target area very narrow at driving distance. The course architect is inviting you to take a chance, but don't be drawn in. Choose a club that lands you short of the trouble, giving you the whole fairway to aim at. You don't lose out because you guarantee an easy second, which in turn should set up a straightforward approach.

EASY TO STAY OUT OF TROUBLE AFTER A GOOD DRIVE

HAZARDS AROUND DRIVING DISTANCE NARROW THE FAIRWAY

LAY UP SHORT OF HAZARDS TO WIDEN TARGET

○ Hit irons off the tee if necessary and be content to keep your ball in play.

As the round progresses, your confidence should rise and the number of serious mistakes fall.

HOW TO SCRAMBLE

Many golfers give in too easily if they strike the ball poorly early in the round. They almost feel that poor form automatically relegates them to a place at the bottom half of the field.

Just because you're hitting the ball poorly, don't think for a minute it's not going to be your day. In-evitably, you're going to find more trouble than you would playing well. But in these situations you have to learn how to scramble, so that you can make the most of your form on the day and come off the course with the lowest score you can manage.

You need to work extra hard at your putting and hope that this is the club that can get you out of jail. It becomes even more crucial to hole those putts for par. And if the chance comes along, grasp birdie opportunities with both hands, because there aren't many up for grabs when you're having a bad day.

Low expectations

Playing golf after a long lay-off – whether as a result of injury or vacation – is probably the one occasion when you can forgive yourself for scoring poorly.

No matter how well you were scoring before the break, you're certain to be a little rusty when you come back. This is likely to be most evident around the greens, so don't expect too much. Try not to get frustrated and disillusioned – the knack of building a score is certain to return if you give it time.

Playing with Better Golfers

One of the great attractions of golf is that you don't have to be a supremely gifted sportsman. You can play, compete with and beat golfers who are better than yourself.

Golf is unique in this respect. Thanks to the handicapping system, Andy Average can wipe the floor with Steve Scratch. There's no greater satisfaction than beating someone who is a better golfer than you. This is part of the thrill of matchplay.

However, many high handicappers are reluctant to play non-competitive games with good golfers – they often feel they're going to make complete fools of themselves on the course.

Don't let embarrassment come between you and what's good for

MIX AND MATCH
Playing against better golfers benefits your game. Try to learn as much as you can from the experience rather than feeling inadequate and wondering why you can't play to the same standard of excellence. With a positive mental approach and thoughtful application, there's no reason why you shouldn't be responsible for your share of giant killings on the golf course.

pro tip

Pace setter

Part of being an accomplished golfer is having the ability to play golf at your own speed while others around you are playing at a different pace altogether. Find a rhythm at which you operate best. Don't vary it under any circumstances, provided of course that you don't upset anyone or hold up play.

This sounds simple, but whether you like it or not, it's easy to drift into – or be influenced by – the pace at which other golfers play the game. This can be quite damaging, because if you play with a golfer who is much slower than you are, you may subconsciously find yourself rushing to avoid holding up the group immediately behind.

If you get involved with a rapid-fire golfer, your swing may tend gradually to quicken as the round goes on, and your game may be in tatters by the end of the day. Fears that you're holding up the quicker members of your group can also speed you up – in the back of your mind you don't want to be called a slowpoke for the rest of your golfing days.

your golf. If you have the opportunity, try to fix up some matches with a couple of quality players. The experience can positively lift your game because their habits rub off on you.

LOOK AND LEARN

Striking ability is often the most eye-catching feature of the good player's game – it's impossible not to sit up and take notice of an impressive ball striker. You can learn a great deal from good striking, not by ball watching, but by picking up on the positive technical points:
○ Lively hands and a solid position through impact.
○ Good rhythm that remains the same for every club in the bag.
○ Impeccable balance throughout.

Try not to feel intimidated by big hitting. This often leads to the high handicapper losing form – usually brought about by an insatiable desire to match every drive and hit the same club into every green.

Play your own game and know your limitations. It's fatal trying to

Avoid making mistakes

In a competitive match, playing against a less accomplished golfer presents you with a good opportunity to display your talents. However, be careful not to become over confident.

As the better player it's absolutely crucial you press home your advantage from the start. Try to give your opponent no sign of hope and make it clear you're not about to give away holes. This pressurizes your opponent into feeling that something special is needed.

keep up with more powerful ball strikers than yourself. It's also not necessary – your higher handicap is designed to counter this imbalance in ability.

The short game is an area where you can pick up some really valuable tips. Good players never have low handicaps purely by chance – they're certain to have a sharp touch around the greens.

While your main concern should always be your own game, try to appreciate how your low handicap partner plays shots from close range. All the fundamentals should be there to see:
○ Hands ahead of the ball at address and through impact.
○ Backswing and followthrough

exactly the same length.
○ A wide range of clubs used from the same range.

If a particular chip shot impresses you, ask what club was used – while you're walking on to the next tee is a suitable opportunity. If you don't feel the time is right to ask questions – just after your partner has missed a short putt perhaps – make sure you look closely at the club and find out for yourself.

Of all the places to discuss certain shots, by far the best is the 19th. Here you have as much time as you like in a friendly and relaxed atmosphere where none of you are wrapped up in your own game.